MAGICKAL
WEDDINGS

MAGICKAL WEDDINGS

Pagan handfasting traditions
for your sacred union

Joy Ferguson

ECW PRESS

The publication of *Magickal Weddings* has been generously supported by the Canada Council for the Arts, which last year invested $20.1 million in writing and publishing throughout Canada, by the Ontario Arts Council, and by the Government of Canada through the Book Publishing Industry Development Program (BPIDP).

CANADIAN CATALOGUING IN PUBLICATION DATA

National Library of Canada Cataloguing in Publication Data.
Ferguson, Joy, 1958.
Magickal weddings: Pagan handfasting traditions for your sacred union
ISBN 978-1-55022-461-0
1. Neopagans—Marriage customs and rites. 2. Marriage customs and rites—
Handbook, manuals, etc. 3. Weddings—Planning—Handbooks, manuals, etc. 1. Title
HQ745.F37 2001   7392'.5'0882999   C2001-900541-5

Front cover illustration by Andrée Charron.
Copyedited by Mary Williams.
Cover and interior design by Guylaine Régimbald—SOLO DESIGN.
This book is set in Truesdell, Campanula, and Papyrus.

Published by ECW PRESS
Suite 200, 2120 Queen Street East
Toronto, Ontario M4E 1E2
416.694.3348 / info@ecwpress.com

ecwpress.com

Printed and bound in Canada

Table of Contents

Dedication &
Acknowledgments

This book is dedicated to Her in all Her guises.

II would like to thank all those at ECWPress who lent their time and expertise to this project. I am particularly grateful to Jack David and Emma McKay.

Sincere thanks, as well, go to my family and friends: Elizabeth and Colin Brown, my children, whose love has supported me in this endeavor and whose creativity was an inspiration; Rob, Liz, and Ryan Ferguson; Amy and Bob Ferguson; Wayne, Robyn, and Sean Cordes; and Cindy Goldrick, Terry Hayes, Jamie Prentice, Sue Simandl, Emily Sinkins and Dawn Zubrisky. Special thanks to Judy Cordes for lending this project her research expertise.

Nature finds no greater delight
Than when two lovers choose to unite.
When spirit, soul, mind and heart
Are joined as one, never to part,
Then Divine energy to this world does flow
To celebrate the union, as above so below.

Introduction

In perfect love and in perfect trust, handfasting couples declare their bond. Handfasting is an intimate expression of lovers' hopes and wishes. And nature is overflowing with magickal traditions and tools to help couples to create the handfasting ceremony that is just right for them. Now, at the dawn of the millennium, more and more people are refusing to be in this world but not of it. They are turning back to nature and seeking to commune with the divine.

When William Wordsworth said, "The world is too much with us," he was lamenting the fact that our burdens have become so overwhelming that we have ceased to see the splendor in life. We run to catch a bus without noticing the sweet smell of the autumn air. We jog along the beach, earphones blasting, ignoring the song of the surf and the feel of warm sand between our toes. We shovel mountains of snow without seeing the ice crystals sparkling in the winter sun.

To know the mystery and magick of the natural world is to be more alive. To sense divinity all around and within is to heighten awareness and experience the richness of everyday life. As we attune ourselves to spirits and forces in the natural world, ritual becomes an expression of this reality.

When a couple handfasts, they acknowledge that their love, a love that mirrors the passions and creativity of the divine, is sacred. Just as the magick in the circle is timeless, so the essence of traditions and rituals does not diminish with age. This book looks back to antiquity to find inspiration for the future.

In Witchcraft in general, and in handfasting in particular, the past offers guidance. But it's not a question of using folklore to validate present experience; in fact, the ancients would insist that Nature herself is a storehouse of wisdom — if you have a question, just ask. It is the essence of Paganism to cross over barriers of time and place, to understand that death is not the end, that our ancestors and their wisdom are accessible. And why not look to the art and architecture, writing and legend, that have been left for us on this side of the veil? To be curious, to question, to explore, to learn, is to connect with the world around us.

As you move through the chapters of this book, you will read about handfasting traditions both old and new. Be inspired. Be creative. Take what is offered here and tailor it to fit your dreams. This handfasting handbook invites lovers to explore the possibilities for the ceremony of their sacred union. It invites couples to create for themselves a magickal day — both figuratively and literally — and to seek the blessing of Nature herself.

When we are handfasted, as we term it, we are man
and wife for a year and a day; that space gone by,
each may choose another mate, or, at their pleasure,
may call the priest to marry them for life,
and this we call handfasting.

—Sir Walter Scott, *The Monastery*

History
& Legality

Handfasting is a ritual that unites two lovers. Whether that union
holds "for a year and a day" or "for as long as their love shall last," the
ceremony has great meaning. The couple's wrists are bound together
with a cord, symbolizing the commitment they have chosen to make.
Tied together, they are as one. When the cords are unbound, the couple remains as one of their own free will.

Today, some couples consider handfasting a form of common-law
marriage, making civil or church ceremonies unnecessary. These couples will renew their vows each year for the rest of their lives, or for as
long as their love endures. Others view the handfasting ceremony as
marking the beginning of an engagement period that will be followed by
a traditional church marriage ceremony. The former view reflects the
pre-Christian status of handfasting; the latter shows how handfasting

has been adapted under the Christian church. Yet, in each instance, the handfasted couple lives the life of married people in the community. Let's explore the origins of this fascinating and lasting tradition.

A HISTORY OF HANDFASTING

Handfasting, as it is practiced today, is most strongly associated with the Ancient Celts, although traditions and elements incorporated into the handfasting ceremony derive from various Pagan cultures and religions. The word *handfasting* comes from the Old English word *han-sælan*, which means to fasten, bind, or tie; the early root of the word, *sal*, means rope.

The *Middle English Dictionary* defines *hond-festen*, or *hand-festen*, as "to betroth (two people), unite; pledge oneself to." As well, the word *wedding* comes from the ancient Anglo-Saxon word *beweddung*, which was the contract to marry made with a verbal promise and a handshake. There is speculation that the handshake is the basis for the *handfast*, but the physical joining of a couple to symbolize their union is common to most early Pagan religions. The *wed* was the initial betrothal payment made at the time of the agreement to handfast — or, in later days, to marry in church.

The spoken word, the oath, was more than a promise. People believed that there was magick in the uttering. Blessings, spells, oaths, and even curses were potent. Greek texts dating from the fourth century B.C.E. contain the word ηχτχδεὼ, "I bind," the magickal phrase in spellcasting. At the time, to break a verbal agreement was to invite dire consequences. Once a couple was betrothed, they were truly in wedlock. Similarly, to plight one's troth — *treowth* means "truth" in Old English — is to take a binding oath.

Written references to handfasting begin in the Middle Ages. This should come as no surprise to us, since the Ancient Celtic culture had an oral tradition. In fact, the Druids considered it irreverent to commit pen to paper — or stylus to tablet. Our understanding of Celtic religion and culture as a whole, then, comes from three sources: archaeology, written sources (classical — non-Celtic — writings and Celtic literature written later, in medieval times), and a wealth of Celtic traditions preserved in practice (such as handfasting, which, of course, has continued well past antiquity). Many of the written sources were influenced by the cultures they came out of and their authors' personal agendas, but they still give us a fascinating glimpse into the world of the Ancient Celts.

And who were the Ancient Celts? When we speak of these people, we are referring to a linguistic group that dominated Central Europe during the Iron Age. The Celts roamed from Asia Minor to Spain, from Egypt through the British Isles, spreading a culture of great spiritual depth.

It is thought that the people of the Hallstatt culture (circa 1000 – 500 B.C.E.) were the earliest Celts. This Early Iron Age community was located near Salzburg, Austria. Excavations at La Téne, in Switzerland, reveal the Celts in their golden age, skillfully crafting iron, evolving a rich oral tradition, and developing unique and powerful art forms; during the fourth century B.C.E., Celtic expansion and influence was at its peak. The burial mounds and other excavations at the La Téne site offer exciting evidence that Celtic tribes traded from the Near East to the Mediterranean to the British Isles.

By the fourth century B.C.E., Celtic warriors bent on seizing the riches of their trading partners were moving southward to attack the Etruscans and the Romans. In about 390 B.C.E., Celtic warriors wearing horned helmets and armed with swords and battleaxes invaded the city of Rome. They would also penetrate Asia Minor and the Near East.

The warfare and migration patterns of the Celts would not only result in the spread of their own culture, but also the assimilation of other cultural influences.

Throughout the first century B.C.E., Julius Caesar and the Romans pushed north towards Britain. This forced the Celts—whom Caesar referred to as the Gauls — to retreat to fortified settlements in Britain and France. The expansion of the Roman Empire put great pressure on the Continental and British Celts to adopt Roman customs and religion. Ireland was never directly impacted by Rome, and so the Irish guarded their Celtic culture more successfully—until Christianity's powerful influence set in.

The Ancient Celts practiced a nature-based religion that revered the Goddess, the Great Earth Mother. Statues and carvings of her dating from 20,000 B.C.E. have been found in the great megalithic structures scattered across Europe. These structures—for example, Stonehenge —

although predating the Ancient Celts, maintained their status as sacred sites. It appears that the Celts absorbed the wisdom—demonstrated by these megalithic structures—of an earlier age and enhanced it with what they learned from the cultures they came into contact with. The wisdom of these people was perpetuated by their art, their sculpture, their architecture, and perhaps even the traditions they handed down beginning millennia ago.

Archaeologists have found artifacts that have helped us to understand the spirituality of the Celts: swords and staffs carved with magickal runes; cauldrons and grails embossed with images of the hunter god, Cernunnos, to name a few. The sacred and powerful folklore of the Celts has come down to us in legends. Perhaps the most powerful Celt legend involves the quest for the Holy Grail and the accounts of

Arthur and Merlin.

The Celts revered Nature, believing her to be a living female entity inhabited by both mortals and spirits. They also believed that no written records were needed, since the natural world itself was a storehouse of knowledge. Because the world was alive, the Celts felt they were always in the presence of the divine. The Spirit dwelled in the smallest acorn and the grandest mountain, yet the physical world was but one existence. The Celts journeyed to other realms through doors unlocked by reverence, ritual, and magick. Their faith in the spiritual and the supernatural made the physical all the more vibrant to the Celts. Creativity and fertility were forces of nature that revealed the divine. The number three was magickal and associated with the Goddess's appearance in the triple guise — maiden, mother, crone — that represented the range of her influence. In the Welsh tradition, Arthur is said to have had three wives, all named Guinevere; this supports the notion that Arthur was a sacred king united to the Goddess in her three guises.

The Celts communed with nature and with their deities through their Druid priests, who performed rituals and practiced divination. From ancient times, the Druids — priests, astrologers, healers, and seers — had formed the Celt intellectual class. They were even powerful enough to bring the Celtic tribes together to rebel against the Romans. Druid initiates served the community and the culture in a secular capacity — as philosophers and judges, historians and teachers. As a priestly upper class, the Druids also maintained the highly ritualistic religion of the Ancient Celts and divined the will of the spirit world for the tribe. Their religion was based on the worship of the Goddess and the God, as well as a multitude of nature deities.

During the Early Middle Ages, as the power of the Roman Empire waned, the Christian church waged a war for the souls of Pagans. The world in which such struggles were taking place was not a world of science. Nature ruled. Popes practiced astrology; herbal remedies restored health more often than the bloodletting of physicians; and the phases of the moon were thought to be signs from the Goddess of what was to occur.

Life was dangerous for the common people of Europe. Robbers and murderers roamed the countryside; disease and famine were everpresent; ogres and trolls threatened children and livestock. People were desperate for a means to protect themselves from all of these earthly and unearthly attacks. The local noble could afford them some protection from human assailants, so small towns sprang up around the lord's castle. But this was not enough. Paganism thrived because the Goddess offered her followers protection in this life and the next.

In rural areas where the Church's influence was weakest, Druidic tradition and Pagan religion continued to flourish. Even in the large towns and cities, the influence of these forces could be seen in the Celtic branch of Christianity that had developed.

In the British Isles, and particularly in Ireland, the Celtic belief in the divinity of nature lasted well into the Middle Ages. A verse from the breastplate of St. Patrick shows the Celt's reverence for the forces of nature as they were accepted into Celtic Christianity:

Today I rise
thanks to the will of Heaven —
fire of the Sun
brilliance of the Moon
glory of Fire
speed of Lightning
swiftness of Wind

depth of Sea
strength of Earth
firmness of Rock.   (Rabey 55)

The rise of Christianity did not eliminate Pagan beliefs. Often, only
a king and his wealthy subjects would convert to the Christian faith,
and even then those subjects would not forego all of Paganism's cultural
and religious elements. Many common people were willing to be bap-
tized — after all, forest groves and lakes were sacred sites for magickal
ceremonies — but in their daily lives they would continue to commune
with the Pagan gods and spirits. To them, the ritual of handfasting remained divinely inspired; as a reenactment of the divine union between
the Goddess and the God, it was far too meaningful to suppress.

The medieval mind was sensitive to visual imagery and adept at
interpreting symbols, so every nuance of the ceremonies and rituals the
medieval Pagan practiced held a wealth of significance. A vital ceremony
such as handfasting was designed to bring the uniting couple and their
families the greatest possible measure of happiness and prosperity. The
time of year for the handfasting would therefore be chosen to harmonize with the rhythms of nature.

The Celtic solar calendar, called The Solar Wheel of the Year (figure
1, page 31), charts the important festivals that honor the gods and goddesses of the Ancient Celtic religion. These festivals mark the cycles of
nature and the resulting changes in village activities. When people lived
close to nature, the changing of the seasons and the cycles of the moon
invited ceremonies of worship and magick in the Goddess's lunar light.

According to the Druidic lore that has come down to us, handfasting
ceremonies were held in a forest grove during one of the Celtic festivals,

Beltane. It would take place around a sacred tree, specially adorned for the ritual, since trees are believed to have mystical qualities. The hawthorn tree, which blooms in May and symbolizes fertility, was a favorite choice for handfasting couples. The Druid priest would lead the couple in a rhythmic dance, raising the energy to unite them, to create their sacred bond, and to generate the forces of passion and fertility. Finally, the Druid would ask the couple to take the vows that would bind them for a year and a day.

The Druid priests would begin the Beltane rites at dusk — a "betwixt and between" time, when magick is potent — and they would last until twilight the following day. The year was perceived to possess a dark half and a light half, and the day was considered a miniature version of this — having a time of light and a time of darkness.

Darkness bred creativity, imagination, and mystery. It was difficult to know what lurked beyond the ring of firelight. Darkness was a time of death, but not eternal death — like the dormant autumn that brings the rebirth of spring. The dark half of the year was from Samhain (October 31) to Beltane, the light half from Beltane to Samhain. The light half of the year was a time to emerge from the darkness of winter into the sunlight of spring. It was a time when all was fresh and vital, a time to be social, a time of unions and new beginnings.

Beltane was a festival of fire. Fire for passion, fire for purity, fire to cleanse any evil that remained after the dark period and to bless the seedling crops, newborn creatures, and young love. On May Eve (April 30), the celebrations involved bonfires and the Druids' magick. The first of May was for maypoles, hawthorn blossoms, and lovemaking.

Today, many people are turning to the ancient traditions once more. Interest in Pagan religions and Witchcraft is growing at a phenomenal rate. Theories abound as to why this is happening, but it seems clear that part of the answer is that people have a renewed desire to partake in traditions that respect both the individual and the natural world. Many have lost hope in our "technologized" society and highly structured religions and are turning back to nature and the spirits who dwell there. They seek a personal communion with the Goddess rather than a divine experience mediated by priests and ministers. They want to take a hands-on approach to life, to regain a sense of personal power in this world. For two lovers, what better expression of freedom is there than choosing to handfast? This ritual draws power from the traditions of the ancients, but it also allows a couple to design a ceremony that is meaningful to them, personally. Whether to be bound by ceremonial oath or legal arrangement — the choice belongs to that couple alone.

THE LEGALITY OF HANDFASTING

In antiquity, the Pagan rites that bound lovers fell under the auspices of the family, not the government. In fact, in one form of union that existed in the Roman Republic, a couple who cohabitated without interruption for a year and a day were considered married by both the state and the community.

As Christianity gained acceptance and began to take hold in Europe, its followers fought to suppress Pagan religion and rituals. In the Early Middle Ages, church weddings were rare, and handfasting prevailed. One medieval document, "Title XXII: How Marriages Should Be Contracted" (1231 A.D.), demonstrates how local lawmakers tried to convince the people that conjugal unions should be recognized by the Christian church:

BY THE PRESENT LAW, WE ORDER THAT ALL THE MEN OF OUR KINGDOM AND ESPECIALLY THE NOBLES WHO DESIRE TO CONTRACT

MARRIAGE MUST HAVE THE MARRIAGE CELEBRATED SOLEMNLY AND
PUBLICLY, WITH DUE SOLEMNITY AND A PRIESTLY BLESSING, AFTER THE
BETROTHAL HAS BEEN SOLEMNIZED. OTHERWISE, THEY SHOULD KNOW
THAT, IF THEY DIE, THEY WOULD BE ACTING AGAINST OUR ROYAL
EDICT AND WOULD HAVE NO LEGITIMATE HEIRS EITHER BY WILL
OR BY INTESTACY AMONG THOSE WHO WERE PROCREATED FROM A
CLANDESTINE AND ILLEGAL MARRIAGE AGAINST OUR LAW. WOMEN
SHOULD ALSO KNOW THAT THEY WOULD HAVE NO LEGAL RIGHT TO
THE DOWERS DUE OTHER WIVES. WE RELAX THE RIGOR OF THIS LAW
TO ALL THOSE WHO HAVE ALREADY CONTRACTED MARRIAGE AT THE
TIME OF ITS PROMULGATION. WE ALSO RELAX THE CHAIN OF THIS
NECESSITY FOR ALL WIDOWS WHO DESIRE TO MARRY A HUSBAND.
(AMT 66)

This law may have been effective locally, but church wedding ceremonies were not conducted throughout Europe in the eleventh century.
At the Synod of Westminster (1200 A.D.), it was ordered that banns —
the public announcement of a couple's intention to unite — be read or
published on three consecutive Sundays. This was upheld by the
Fourth Lateran Council (1215 A.D.). And it wasn't until the fourteenth
century that church weddings became more commonplace, although
often the wedding consisted of no more than a priest's blessing at the
door of the church.

The fact that the Church had to fight to define and control sacred
unions bolsters the historical evidence that the practice of handfasting
endured. The following excerpts from a series of medieval texts illus-
trates how the Church strove to legislate what people were refusing
to do voluntarily. The excerpted phrases contain veiled references to
handfasting — for example, "Clandestine marriages" — lending further

support to the idea that handfasting was widespread.

1. One man may not take (in marriage) a girl betrothed
   to another man . . .
2. If a man plights his troth to any woman, he is not permitted to
   marry another . . .
3. Clandestine marriages should not be made . . .
4. It is not permitted to perform a marriage in secret . . .
5. No one shall marry a wife without a public ceremony . . .

(Amt 80)

The Church dictated the behavior it wanted, but few listened because the institution was not yet well enough entrenched to wield such authority. But once Christianity became an accepted belief system and excommunication became a tangible threat, the Church's power became real. In 1545, a religious council was held at Trent. Its challenge was to reinstate the doctrines of the Roman Catholic Church — the Reformation had taken its toll. By 1563, the Council of Trent had declared that marriages not performed as a religious sacrament were illegal. Unions were to be conducted in the presence of a priest and two witnesses. With this decree, the popularity of church weddings surged. Still, handfasting was not wiped out; those who sought a compromise established the tradition of handfasting as an engagement ceremony.

Today, handfasting is enjoying a strong revival. The modern handfasting ceremony is a meaningful alternative to a legal marriage for those whose lifestyle, philosophy, or religion welcomes Nature's blessing of their union. Also, an important part of handfasting's appeal is its communal aspect. A handfasting couple — like couples who marry in various kinds of ceremonies — stand before their friends, relatives, and community, accepting their recognition and support.

But it's important for the handfasting couple to remember that the meaningful, nature-oriented, community-affirmed ceremony they have chosen may have no legal status. And a legal union is the essential basis for resolving such key issues as the division of property, child custody, taxes, and inheritance. Some couples may feel that common-law or "marriage-like" legal status is all they require, but it is essential that they think it through carefully before deciding. After all, they will be entering into a financial partnership as well as a loving union.

If you are planning to participate, with your partner, in a handfasting but want your union to have legal status, keep in mind that matrimonial law differs from state to state, province to province, country to country. Furthermore, it's an area of the law that is evolving rapidly. Gender and equality issues continue to be debated, resulting in the revision of existing legislation. To research the laws that are in force in your area, start with the attorney general's office; phone or, better yet, check its Web site. From here, you may be sent to municipal sites for a listing of license issuers.

In most cases, a handfasting ceremony is only legally binding when it is performed by an ordained minister. This may not be as great an obstacle as you might imagine. Check handfasting Web sites for a directory of ordained ministers licensed to perform handfastings that will have legal status. When you've completed this step, confirm the information you've gathered with your local authorities.

It is worth noting that in many parts of the United States even common-law or "marriage-like" unions do not automatically confer marital status. Generally speaking, to be awarded legal status in the United States, a common-law union must meet the following three requirements: the couple must be heterosexual; the couple must present themselves to the community as a married couple, filing their taxes, for example, in a joint return; and the couple must have the intention of getting legally married in the near future.

Although there are bills pending to amend the marriage laws, the states currently recognizing common-law unions with some of the rights and obligations of marital status are: Alabama, Colorado, the District of Columbia, Iowa, Kansas, Montana, New Hampshire (partially), Oklahoma, Pennsylvania, Rhode Island, South Carolina, Texas, and Utah.

In the Province of Newfoundland, the registrar general may register a person to solemnize a marriage. That person will be granted the powers of a marriage registrar, so long as he or she meets certain requirements. The intent behind this rule seems to be to make it possible for members of less-well-established faiths to marry in a ceremony that suits their belief systems. Such a ceremony may be tailored to a couple's individual needs, as long as that couple declares, at some point in the ritual, that they know of no lawful impediment to their being joined, swear that they intend to enter into their union in love and faith, and ask those present to witness the event. The exact wording for these declarations may be obtained from the Ministry of the Attorney General of Newfoundland and Labrador.

In the Province of Ontario, a civil marriage must be performed by a justice of the peace (or a judge), but a ritual ceremony may be conducted by any person who is recognized by a religious organization and registered, under the Marriage Act, to officiate at marriages. There are several Internet sites through which you may contact ministers of different faiths and spiritual associations who are willing and able to perform handfastings. Your union may also be solemnized under the authority of a marriage license or the publication of banns, depending on the denomination — but there are some obstacles to this course of action, particularly for same-sex couples.

In the Province of British Columbia, matrimonial law has been up-dated to address "registered domestic partners." The Domestic Partner Act allows for a couple to make a joint declaration that they are domes-tic partners and as such request the status of married spouses. The act goes on to outline what rights and obligations may derive from this declaration. No ceremony is necessary; all that's required is, simply, a legal document, so the handfasting can be designed without restrictions.

Once you've researched and resolved the legal questions arising from your decision to handfast, you will be free to take the next step: setting the date.

Rise up, my love, my fair one, and come away.
For, lo, the winter is past,
the rain is over and gone . . . .

— The Song of Songs

Timing:
When to Handfast

You have the whole year to choose from. How do you decide which day is the very best on which to handfast? For the ancient Pagans, the decision was a complicated one. Deities were omnipresent. The seasons were expressions of the divine powers. The natural world was imbued with magick. Only by interpreting a complex network of signs in nature could a couple—with the help of a Druid priest or an astrologer— choose an auspicious time to handfast.

THE MONTH TO HANDFAST

The Celtic year is divided into a dark half and a light half. The dark half of the year is a time of creativity, a time when physical life is dormant but magickal and spiritual forces thrive. It is a period for imagining and planning. The light half of the year sees a bursting forth of those ideas into the light of the sun. It is a social time, when plans are brought to fruition.

One myth of months and seasons has it that the dark portion of the year is heralded by the death of the God, the sun; this occurs on October 31, and it marks Samhain, the most important Ancient Celtic festival. Samhain is considered to be "outside of time," when the veil between reality and the spirit realm grows thinnest. Nature readies herself for winter, the magickal oak pulls its sap back down to its roots, the days become shorter, and the God withdraws. But he does not fall into an eternal sleep — in fact, the dark half of the year is a time of great creativity, spirituality, and divine magick, as the God is reborn in the womb of the Goddess. She — as Moon Goddess, as Mother — nurtures him through the dark autumn until December 21, the winter solstice, when, in the northern hemisphere, the night is longest and the day shortest. On that day, the Goddess gives birth to her son. The God's birth is considered a joyous occasion, a time of new beginnings. And so the tradition arose in Scotland and Ireland to announce a betrothal — or sometimes even to hold a handfast — in late December or early January.

As the days grow longer, so the Sun God grows stronger. Celtic festivals celebrate his developing maturity and its reflection in the greening landscape. Finally, at Beltane, the God reaches manhood, inaugurating the light half of the year. The Moon Goddess, as maiden, becomes his lover and mate. Their passion is afire in nature; the earth is infused with their fertility. In the ancient world, Beltane was a popular time to handfast, because then the handfasting couple could be fired by the energies of the Goddess and the God.

On August 1, the festival of Lughnasadh, the first harvest, gets underway. This is the time to reap what has been sown. The God is in full manhood, the Goddess is with child. The Christians of the Middle Ages often chose Lughnasadh as a day to wed, a day to harvest the love sown during the handfast.

The fall equinox, September 21, is the period when storehouses are full from the harvest. It is a time of plenty. Since in September there is often a glorious harvest moon, this time of year is also equated with fertility, and it is therefore another favorable moment for loving unions. And, as summer turns to fall, the cycle of death and rebirth begins again.

Figure 1: The Solar Wheel of the Year

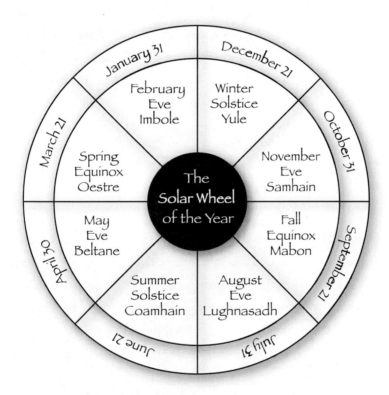

The most popular time of the year to handfast in Celtic antiquity was May. Imagine the unspoiled English countryside bursting to life in the spring. Fields of fragrant lavender, wild roses climbing wood-fence borders, the perfume of apple blossoms wafting through the sunlit air, the mighty groves of oak crowned with fresh green foliage. To the Celtic Pagans, spring was magickal, the season when the veils separating our world and the spirit world could be penetrated. The Celtic myths that characterize each month have symbolic depth; any given segment of the Solar Wheel may give rise to the kind of symbolism that reflects the spirit of your union. Still, there is a compelling tradition to support the notion that May, perhaps even Beltane, is the most wonderful time to handfast.

The festival of Beltane starts at twilight on the eve of April 30 and continues until dusk on May 1. The Ancient Celts believed that at Beltane the Goddess and the God united; so, in their honor, couples would "go a maying" in the faery woods, which were rife with spirits. They would gather boughs of the hawthorn (also called "the may") — the tree that symbolized courtship and love — and build bonfires to represent divine passion. Maypoles were erected and decorated with ribbons and flowers, again to symbolize the union of the Goddess and the God.

Many a handfast was initiated at Beltane and renewed the next year at the Beltane fire. In fact, the word *honeymoon* comes from this time. Meade, a sweet ale made from fermented honey, was considered a delectable gift from the gods. It was prepared for the Beltane celebrations and likely consumed at handfastings from the full moon in May until the full moon in June. This interval between full moons became known as the "meade moon," or "honeymoon."

It would seem, then, after consulting the Solar Wheel of the Year and considering the rich tradition and symbolism encompassed by Beltane, that the choice of when to handfast is quite straightforward. But we still haven't taken one crucial factor into account: astrology.

Probably the most impressive megalithic site in Europe is a double ring of eighty stone pillars set on Salisbury Plain in the south of England. This prehistoric sanctuary attests to the ancients' reverence for the celestial bodies and their movement through the heavens. In the Middle Ages, the people of Europe were influenced by the zodiac of the Romans (Aries through Pisces) and the lunar astrology of the Druids. So profoundly influenced were they that couples relied on astrology to help them decide when to marry.

The popularity and legitimacy of astrology in the Middle Ages is often underestimated. In fact, the University of Bologna — where Dante studied — established a chair of astrology in 1125 A.D. Over a century later, St. Thomas Aquinas declared that astrology complemented Church doctrine. Pope Sixtus IV (1414–1484) was the first pope to construct and interpret horoscopes. And, of course, Nostradamus (1503–1566) enjoyed fame and royal favor.

In Celtic astrology, a specific tree (or bush or vine) is linked to each of the lunar cycles that the ancients identified. Because the Druids possessed an intimate understanding of nature's mystical qualities, the association of trees with divinity and magickal properties was a natural evolution. The Tree of Life was first mentioned five thousand years ago, in Near Eastern myth (the Ancient Celts traded in the Near East), but the image of the tree is found in most religions as a symbol of fertility, rejuvenation, and immortality. Because trees unite the sky (the God) and the earth (the Goddess), they harbor a great magickal power. The Druids assigned a tree to each cycle of the moon and recorded the quality of the natural energy during that time period. The value of tree astrology to the individual, then, is as a means of understanding the energies alive in nature at any given time of the year.

When we are planning any important event, it is essential for us to work in harmony with the forces of nature. So, as a couple preparing to handfast, you should choose a time for your ceremony when the qualities you value in your union, as represented by a special tree, are active in the natural world. Traditionally, the elder is the least favored tree, and the hawthorn is the most favored. There has been much debate over the various uses and representations of Druid astrology; it is a complex system of divination. For those whose main purpose is selecting a handfasting month, however, the Celtic Lunar/Tree Astrology Wheel (figure 2) may contain all the necessary information.

Figure 2: Celtic Lunar/Tree Astrology Wheel

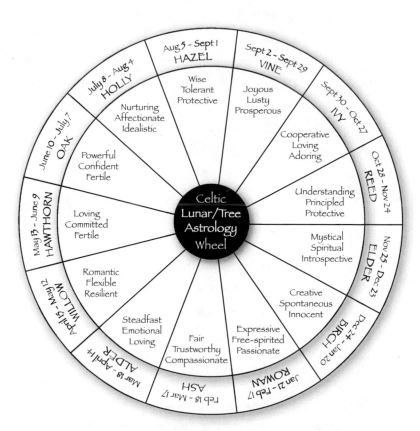

You may find that the understanding of tree astrology offered by the wheel will also enrich other aspects of your handfasting: if you plan to jump the broom, you could make a besom (or add to an existing broom) using twigs from your chosen tree; if your ceremony allows for an open fire or a roaring fireplace or even some decorative torches, you could tie together a bundle of those twigs (or even a mixture of twigs from several appropriate tree varieties) to burn as a symbol of your wish to have certain qualities in your union.

If, having chosen a month to handfast based on the Solar Wheel of the Year and Celtic tree astrology, you want further confirmation of your choice, then extend your investigation a little further. You could look to the astrology of the Near East and the Mediterranean — the Aries-to-Pisces zodiac so familiar to present-day North Americans — which was practiced widely during the Middle Ages. The signs of the zodiac and the planets have meanings that either harmonize with or offer a challenge to our individual aspirations. There are now Internet sites that offer complimentary chart construction. You can create a chart for the time that you wish to handfast and then study the general indications. Use birth-chart information, along with the other elements, such as lunar phases, to determine the most auspicious time to celebrate a prosperous, happy, and enduring union.

The Zodiac Signs and Rulership chart (figure 3, page 36) presents some general guidelines. Look for a gathering of celestial bodies in Libra or Taurus — both ruled by Venus, the planet that signifies love. A May date should give you two or more planets in Taurus. Cancer, the sign that signifies fertility, is also favorable. A strong Scorpio influence, or a gathering of planets in Scorpio, should be avoided, as should the influences of Capricorn and Aquarius.

Figure 3: Zodiac Signs and Rulership

ZODIAC SIGN	RULING PLANET	DATE
Aries	Mars	March 20 – April 20
Taurus	Venus	April 20 – May 20
Gemini	Mercury	May 20 – June 20
Cancer	Moon	June 20 – July 20
Leo	Sun	July 20 – Aug. 20
Virgo	Mercury	Aug. 20 – Sept. 20
Libra	Venus	Sept.20 – Oct. 20
Scorpio	Pluto	Oct.20 – Nov. 20
Sagittarius	Jupiter	Nov.20 – Dec. 20
Capricorn	Saturn	Dec. 20 – Jan. 20
Aquarius	Uranus	Jan.20 – Feb.20
Pisces	Neptune	Feb. 20 – March 20

*The sun does not always enter a zodiac sign precisely on the twentieth of the month. An ephemeris will confirm the date and time between the eighteenth and the twenty-second.

THE DAY TO HANDFAST

Celtic festivals, such as Beltane, take place on the eve and the following day. Again, this spanning of the dark and light halves of the day symbolizes the dark-to-light cycle of the year. And, just as Beltane and Samhain occurred on the special days when the light and dark halves of the year met, so twilight and dawn were "betwixt and between" periods when magick was potent and the spiritual world was veiled very thinly. Out of this arose the tradition of avoiding dusk and dawn as a time to hold a handfasting ceremony, and, in fact, an old Irish proverb asserts that if the sun shines on a couple, then good fortune will, as well.

To better understand the importance of choosing the right day to handfast, we must turn to astrology once more. Ancient astrologers held that each day of the week was ruled by one particular celestial body (out of this belief grew the designations for the days of the week that we use today). Traditionally, Monday or Friday — that is, Moon's Day or Venus's Day — are considered the best days to handfast (but, as you will notice when you look at The Rulership of Hours (figure 7, pages 44-45), if one focuses on choosing the correct hour to handfast, then any day becomes a possibility).

Figure 4: The Theory of Planetary Days

LATIN	SAXON	ENGLISH
Sol	Sun's day	Sunday
Luna	Moon's day	Monday
Martis (Mars)	Tiw's day	Tuesday
Mercurius	Woden's day	Wednesday
Jove (Jupiter)	Thor's day	Thursday
Veneris (Venus)	Frigg's day	Friday
Saturni	Seterne's day	Saturday

The next step in selecting an ideal day to handfast is taking a close look at lunar cycles. We cannot underestimate their importance. The moon, moving through the heavens, was the premier timing device for astrologer-priests in all ancient agricultural civilizations. So dominant is the moon's time symbolism that even today our calendar months are roughly based on that astral body's trek through the zodiac. In fact, the word *month* comes from the Anglo-Saxon *mona*, meaning *moon*. And, of course, *Monday* is the Saxon term for *Moon's Day*.

It is difficult for us to comprehend just how awesome the phases of the moon were to ancient stargazers. They believed that the Moon Goddess, through her shapeshifting, heralded the time to sow, the time to reap, and even the time to handfast. Each phase of the moon symbolized specific energies. Just as the moon caused the oceans to rise and fall, its phases were thought to control the tide of worldly events.

In pre-Christian times, there was no Man in the Moon, but there was a powerful Goddess. In her persona as Earth Mother, she was worshipped across time and space, from ancient Babylon to Celtic Europe: as Selene in Greece, as Isis in Egypt, and as Boann in Ireland. In the oldest cultures, the power of the moon to influence people's daily lives was viewed as greater than that of the sun, the other great luminary. Since the Goddess nurtured fertility and the cycles of nature, her favor was essential to any agricultural people.

The feminine principle — ruled by instinct, emotion, empathy, creativity, fertility, love, passion, inspiration, and selfless giving — was not merely tolerated by the entire culture of men and women, it was celebrated. But, as civilizations organized and commerce grew in towns and cities, the qualities of the sun, the God — who controlled rather than influenced, reasoned rather than intuited, possessed rather than shared, and ruled the physical world of daylight rather than the spiritual world of darkness — took on greater and greater significance. With this shift in emphasis there was a shift in values, but the cult of the Moon Goddess and its worship of feminine principles would continue to hold sway in some quarters. Devotees kept the Goddess's power alive. Because of this, couples today are studying the phases of the moon to determine which day they should handfast.

Handfasting during a new moon is becoming popular, because of the notion that a new moon heralds new beginnings. Yet it isn't quite as simple as that. If you are considering handfasting at the new moon in order to capture the energies of this emotional and exuberant moment, remember that it marks the beginning of the lunation cycle. Change will follow. You and your partner will need to be very open with each other so that you can shape these energies and release them in a positive way; and, as a couple, you will need to be very adaptable. By choosing to have your union symbolized by excitement and unpredictability, you become bound by energies that are not only lusty and passionate, but also undisciplined and unfocused.

Instead, why not allow the new moon to symbolize the beginning of your commitment to handfast? Lunar energies are much better directed towards releasing romantic love for all the world to see. In fact, the new moon is the ideal time to begin this most important journey. It is a time when deep emotions are stirred. The energies of the new moon fuel us with creativity and inspire us to initiate new projects. Because new-moon energies are spontaneous and vibrant, they lead us to be innovative and imaginative. The new phase of the moon is the ideal time to declare your intent to handfast and to begin planning. One option you may consider is announcing your handfasting at the new moon in January and setting the ceremony for the full moon in May.

The new moon takes approximately two weeks to wax to its fullest each month. As it does, your plans and intentions will clarify. The energies of a waxing moon move plans forward nicely. As more and more light shines down on us, it illuminates the truth of our intentions. Study New Moons — Dates for 2001-2009 (figures 5 and 6, pages 40-43) to see which coming new moon coincides with your other date-selection criteria.

At the new moon, announce to your friends that you will handfast and begin to plan.

Figure 5: New Moon ● Dates for 2001-2009

2001	2002	2003
January 24	January 13	January 2
February 23	February 12	February 1
March 25	March 14	March 3
April 23	April 12	April 1
May 23	May 12	May 1
June 21	June 10	May 31
July 20	July 10	June 29
August 19	August 8	July 29
September 17	September 7	August 27
October 16	October 6	September 26
November 15	November 4	October 25
December 14	December 4	November 23
		December 23

2004	2005	2006
January 21	January 10	January 29
February 20	February 8	February 28
March 20	March 10	March 29
April 19	April 8	April 27
May 19	May 8	May 27
June 17	June 6	June 25
July 17	July 6	July 25
August 16	August 5	August 23
September 14	September 3	September 22
October 14	October 3	October 22
November 12	November 2	November 20
December 12	December 1	December 20
	December 31	

2007	2008	2009
January 19	January 8	January 26
February 17	February 7	February 25
March 19	March 7	March 26
April 17	April 6	April 25
May 16	May 5	May 24
June 15	June 3	June 22
July 14	July 3	July 22
August 12	August 1	August 20
	August 30	
September 11	September 29	September 18
October 11	October 28	October 18
November 9	November 27	November 16
December 9	December 27	December 16

At the full moon, the Goddess is at the height of her power and influence. Symbolically, her cycle, which was initiated at the new moon, reaches its apex when the moon waxes full. The positive energy of the full moon makes it a desirable time to handfast. Beneath a full moon, relationships can reach their full potential; partners give and share; emotions achieve a balance, and a sense of security prevails.

If the full moon is a time when new energies mature and grow to their culmination, then the time between the full moon and new moon, when the moon's light wanes, is a quiet interval in which to appreciate what one has accomplished. The waning moon is a time of introspection, a period for enjoying the rewards that came to fruition with the full moon. Symbolically, the time between the full moon and new moon, as the moon wanes, is not a good time to handfast. The outward energy of the moon is in decline. Plans and commitments made during this waning period are more likely to be frustrated.

At the full moon, perform the handfasting ceremony.

Figure 6: Full Moon ⬤ Dates for 2001-2009

2001	2002	2003
January 9	January 28	January 18
February 8	February 27	February 16
March 9	March 28	March 18
April 8	April 27	April 16
May 7	May 26	May 16
June 6	June 24	June 14
July 5	July 24	July 13
August 4	August 22	August 12
September 2	September 21	September 10
October 2	October 21	October 10
November 1	November 20	November 9
November 30	December 19	December 8
December 30		

2004	2005	2006
January 7	January 25	January 14
February 6	February 24	February 13
March 6	March 25	March 14
April 5	April 24	April 13
May 4	May 23	May 13
June 3	June 22	June 11
July 2	July 21	July 11
July 31	August 19	August 9
August 30	September 18	September 7
September 28	October 17	October 7
October 28	November 16	November 5
November 26	December 15	December 5
December 26		

2007	2008	2009
January 3	January 22	January 11
February 2	February 21	February 9
March 3	March 21	March 11
April 2	April 20	April 9
May 2	May 20	May 9
June 1	June 18	June 7
June 30	July 18	July 7
July 30	August 16	August 6
August 28	September 15	September 4
September 26	October 14	October 4
October 26	November 13	November 2
November 24	December 12	December 2
December 24		December 31

THE HOUR TO HANDFAST

In antiquity, only five planets and the sun and moon were visible. It was the Egyptians who first listed these celestial bodies according to their apparent traveling speed: Saturn, Jupiter, Mars, the sun, Venus, Mercury, and the moon. Each was granted rulership over a specific day. This meant that, beginning at sunrise, a day's first hour was influenced by its namesake planet. Rulership then followed in the order listed in The Rulership of Hours (figure 7, pages 43-44). Once seven hours had passed, the cycle would begin again. Each planet and luminary was also assigned rulership over a different area of life and aspect of the world.

As you start to count the hours to determine the time of your handfasting, you will discover that you can schedule the ceremony to be under the influence of Venus or the moon on any day of the week.

For example, a Saturday handfasting scheduled for either about 10 a.m. or 5 p.m. would be influenced by Venus; and even if you're running late or long, your ceremony will still fall under the benevolent influences of Mercury or the moon. Try to avoid the planets Mars and Saturn; they exert negative energies.

Figure 7: The Rulership of Hours

	Sun	Venus	Mercury	Moon	Saturn	Jupiter	Mars
Sun Sunday			1 a.m.	2 a.m.	3 a.m.	4 a.m.	5 a.m.
	6 a.m.	7 a.m.	8 a.m.	9 a.m.	10 a.m.	11 a.m.	noon
	1 p.m.	2 p.m.	3 p.m.	4 p.m.	5 p.m.	6 p.m.	7 p.m.
	8 p.m.	9 p.m.	10 p.m.	11 p.m.	mid.		
Moon Monday						1 a.m.	2 a.m.
	3 a.m.	4 a.m.	5 a.m.	6 a.m.	7 a.m.	8 a.m.	9 a.m.
	10 a.m.	11 a.m.	noon	1 p.m.	2 p.m.	3 p.m.	4 p.m.
	5 p.m.	6 p.m.	7 p.m.	8 p.m.	9 p.m.	10 p.m.	11 p.m.
	mid.						
Mars Tuesday		1 a.m.	2 a.m.	3 a.m.	4 a.m.	5 a.m.	6 a.m.
	7 a.m.	8 a.m.	9 a.m.	10 a.m.	11 a.m.	noon	1 p.m.
	2 p.m.	3 p.m.	4 p.m.	5 p.m.	6 p.m.	7 p.m.	8 p.m.
	9 p.m.	10 p.m.	11 p.m.	mid.			
Mercury Wednesday					1 a.m.	2 a.m.	3 a.m.
	4 a.m.	5 a.m.	6 a.m.	7 a.m.	8 a.m.	9 a.m.	10 a.m.
	11 a.m.	noon	1 p.m.	2 p.m.	3 p.m.	4 p.m.	5 p.m.
	6 p.m.	7 p.m.	8 p.m.	9 p.m.	10 p.m.	11 p.m.	mid.

	Sun	Venus	Mercury	Moon	Saturn	Jupiter	Mars
Jupiter	1 a.m.	2 a.m.	3 a.m.	4 a.m.	5 a.m.	7 a.m.	7 a.m.
Thursday	8 a.m.	9 a.m.	10 a.m.	11 a.m.	noon	1 p.m.	2 p.m.
	3 p.m.	4 p.m.	5 p.m.	6 p.m.	7 p.m.	8 p.m.	9 p.m.
	10 p.m.	11 p.m.	mid.				
				1 a.m.	2 a.m.	3 a.m.	4 a.m.
Venus	5 a.m.	6 a.m.	7 a.m.	8 a.m.	9 a.m.	10 a.m.	11 a.m.
Friday	noon	1 p.m.	2 p.m.	3 p.m.	4 p.m.	5 p.m.	6 p.m.
	7 p.m.	8 p.m.	9 p.m.	10 p.m.	11 p.m.	mid.	
							1 a.m.
Saturn	2 a.m.	3 a.m.	4 a.m.	5 a.m.	6 a.m.	7 a.m.	8 a.m.
Saturday	9 a.m.	10 a.m.	11 a.m.	noon	1 p.m.	2 p.m.	3 p.m.
	4 p.m.	5 p.m.	6 p.m.	7 p.m.	8 p.m.	9 p.m.	10 p.m.
	11 p.m.	mid.					

SETTING THE TIME

Now that you've explored the symbolism inherent in months, days, and times, you can use the information to arrive at a decision about exactly when to handfast. Here are seven steps you may choose to follow:

1. Begin by considering what astrology tells us about the months of the year. You have the qualities of the popular zodiac (Aries through Pisces) to work with, as well as the Celtic Lunar/Tree Astrology Wheel (figure 2, page 31), which details the attributes assigned to various times of the year. Find three months that have

the attributes you wish for in your union. Write these down on the Timing Choices chart (figure 8, page 47).

2. Reread the portions of this chapter that discuss the energies active under a new moon and under a full moon. Decide which phases you prefer. Enter your three choices on the chart.

3. Look at the lists of dates under the moon phases you have chosen (figures 5 and 6, pages 40-43). Find the three months you selected in the first step of this process. Enter the dates of the corresponding full or new moons on the chart.

4. Now use The Theory of Planetary Days (figure 4, page 37) to determine the meaning of the days of the week on which your dates fall. With a full moon, times up to two days before the date listed in the figure are still potent. With a new moon, times up to two days after retain a vibrant energy. There are good reasons to choose dates that fall during the waxing rather than the waning of the moon. Enter the days you have selected on the chart.

5. Now turn to The Rulership of Hours (figure 7, page 44). Review the information on zodiacal influences, or choose hours that correspond to Venus or the moon. Enter these on the chart.

6. You now have a Timing Choices chart listing the month, day, and time of each of your three choices. (Should you wish to refine your selection process a little more, skip ahead and read chapter 5, Sacred Space and Divination, and then add a column to the Timing Choices chart that records the messages you receive when divining.)

7. Finally, review any practical considerations you may have, such as site availability or the schedules of your guests. You are now ready to make your ultimate choice of the month, day, and hour to handfast.

Figure 8: Timing Choices

	Month	Phase	Dates	Weekday	Hour	Divination	Comments
First Choice							
Second Choice							
Third Choice							

In the ancient and medieval worlds of the Celts and the Europeans, visual symbolism was the language of ideas and communication. Nature was alive with spirits and deities, meanings and messages could be found in a twig or in the hour of the day, and the timing of such an important event as a sacred union was a matter of great import and precision. A couple who united harmoniously with the forces of nature was believed to be destined for happiness and prosperity. By employing the wisdom of those worlds to set your time to handfast, you will be sharing in a potent and enduring tradition.

God is in the details.

—Ludwig Mies van der Rohe

Planning Your Handfasting Ceremony and Celebration

In other sections of this book, we explore the romantic meaning of your special day. In this chapter, we get practical. For your handfasting, you are the project manager. If you take the time to organize yourself and to guide your friends gently towards performing certain tasks for you, you will find that the day of your handfasting ceremony will proceed smoothly and that you will be able to relax and enjoy it.

Can there be so much to plan? Yes there can, but don't allow yourself to be intimidated by it. And don't be intimidated by the size of this chapter. Your ceremony and celebration may need much less planning than is covered here — but do read through these pages, anyway. This chapter will help you to make sure that all the details are taken care of; you don't want to be running around at your own celebration in search of an extra ten forks and a bottle opener!

Often, handfasting couples envision a simple ceremony, attended by about twenty close friends, and followed by a celebration. But be careful. Those twenty friends will want to bring their significant others. The celebration will involve toasting and feasting. Eventually, a soundtrack will slip into the daydream images you have of your handfasting and, before you know it, the whole thing will get out of hand. You need to plan. Forty people who are going to eat and drink will need glasses and utensils, not to mention ice and cocktail cherries. You may not be serving Manhattans, but the point is that many small details will crop up that, if overlooked, will leave you frantic on your special day.

Allow yourself plenty of time to plan. If you are organizing a simple handfasting and celebration at your home for fewer than fifty people, give yourself a minimum of three months. If you will be welcoming more than fifty, you could need as much as a year, depending on the availability of the facility you want to rent. Generally, if you announce your handfasting at the new moon in January and then schedule the ceremony for the full moon in May, you will have lots of time to make all of your decisions and organize a simple yet meaningful event.

This chapter provides you with a list of decisions you'll need to make as well as a budget worksheet and a celebration choreography. Each decision will have an impact on every other decision, so remain flexible during the months it will take you to decide and plan. For example, you may realize halfway through creating the budget worksheet that you simply cannot manage this event in your own apartment. You must then either ask a friend or family member if you can use their house, or look into renting space. If you choose to handfast outdoors, be sure to arrange and budget for a rain-day backup locale.

Once you complete the worksheet, you still need to be adaptable. There will be changes, but if you have been organized from the outset, these changes won't alter the framework that you have already set.

Remember that this day belongs to you as a couple. Share in the decisions listed here and adapt to the changes together.

DECISIONS

The first decision that you must make is how much to spend on your celebration. Don't let yourself be pushed to exceed this figure. Establish what you and/or your parents can afford and do not allow negative feelings to mar your handfast because you have become financially burdened by your choices. Keep in mind that this is the beginning of your commitment to each other, and there will be plenty of other things to spend your money on—a house, a vacation, a car. Settle on a reasonable dollar figure for your handfasting, and don't lose sight of it.

The second decision you'll need to make is how many guests to invite. Don't guess at a number, draw up a list. Thirty names will quickly become fifty as you realize that so-and-so will be hurt if he or she is not included.

Once you know how much you have to spend and how many people will be coming, you can begin to answer the when/where questions. You have determined the most meaningful time for you, as a couple, to handfast, and now you face the challenge of making the event a practical reality. At first, the decisions you have to make will seem endless: Will friends who live a plane trip away be more likely to attend if you set the handfasting at an off-peak travel time? If an outdoor celebration is what you desire, can you obtain a permit to hold it in a park on your chosen day? Is the hall you want to rent or the friend's house you want to use available? If you are using a donated location, such as your parents' home, do you have time to do the necessary touch-ups (gardening, painting)? Does your chosen location allow candles, torches, or whatever elements you plan to include in the ceremony? Can you get a liquor license for the location? Will your chair-rental firm set up outdoors? Is there a sufficient power supply for the DJ? Can you set up a platform for the soloist you've hired so that her instrument will be protected from the damp earth? What are the cleanup requirements, and by what time must the cleanup be completed?

On it goes. It is important to allow yourself enough time to make these decisions as well as any arrangements that become necessary. You must also give your guests plenty of notice so that they can make their own plans (or even lend a hand). One effective way to organize and address the multitude of decisions that confront you is to group them in categories. Here is an alphabetical list of those categories and a few tips to help you get started.

Attire

Traditionally, how you, the couple, choose to dress dictates the level of formality for the day. Many couples who handfast opt for a Celtic theme and dress accordingly. They invite their guests to do the same, and thereby create a theme handfasting. But this is your day, so feel free to choose whatever appeals to you — from street clothes to conventional formal wear. Just remember, though, that it will be a long day, so you should select comfortable attire. Also, keep in mind that you will be turned away from your guests for much of the ceremony; you might want to wear something with interesting details on the back. One more practical suggestion: buy your shoes a couple of months in advance and wear them around the house to break them in.

Cake

If you have invited many guests, it won't be practical for you and your partner to stand at the cake table for an hour, cutting and serving.

Instead, the two of you can make the ceremonial cut, and then step away from the table. Have helpers on hand. If the cake is tiered, one helper must quickly take it apart (placing the top layer in a safe place so that you can freeze it and enjoy it on your first anniversary; remember that it must have alcohol in it, or it will not survive a year in the freezer). In the meantime, another helper should mark out a checker-board pattern on the cake. Then the organized serving may begin. If your event includes a sit-down meal, then cake can be served to guests at their tables; if you're having a buffet, then guests can line up at the cake table. Cutting and serving the cake can be an awkward task, so don't leave the job to one person. If you are using a caterer, ask if there is a per-slice cake-cutting fee.

Color

The first big color question is, how can you combine the colors that have meaning for your union into a beautiful decor scheme? Although a rainbow of colors might symbolize your aspirations, there is no need to use such a palette in every aspect of your ceremony. The overall impression you create for those who have come to celebrate with you is an important consideration, and a circus-like array of colors could send the wrong message.

One simple solution is to choose a key element and use it to convey your symbolic color choices — the cake, or a centerpiece basket of herbs and flowers. For the ritual itself, take the color of greatest signifi-cance, then add two other colors for accents. For example — letting na-ture be your guide — select the gorgeous pink of a rose and accent it with white and a rich green. These colors can be worked into the decor of the celebration, the decorations, your attire, and the ceremonial tools; also, varieties of flowers symbolic of the meaning you seek to convey can be used in the ceremony. And don't forget gold and silver. Little touches here and there — candlesticks, a vase, a ceremonial dagger, ceremonial wine goblets — add sparkle in candlelight without undermining the color scheme.

Every color comes in a multitude of shades. Go to your local paint store and borrow (for a small, refundable deposit) a book of chips. Take it home and examine the samples in various lights, including candlelight. When you have narrowed down your color choices, look at the individual chips side-by-side, and then hold them against a white wall. Remember that colors change not only in certain lights, but also when placed next to a lighter or darker color. Keep in mind, as well, that you don't need very much of a dark color to make an impact: for instance, if you have found a wonderful marine blue that truly speaks to you, ask yourself whether it would be right for a whole wall in your home or just a border. The answer to that question will help you to decide whether your handfasting gown should be blue with white ribbons or white with blue ribbons. Finally, consider the fact that if you choose an unusual color, you will have trouble finding the perfect match for all of your accessories; that is, it is unlikely that the precise shade of your marine-blue paint chip will be replicated in your dress fabrics, ribbons, candles, and serviettes. Be practical. Play with colors until you find a combination that is not only lovely and meaningful to you as a couple, but also readily available.

Contracts

Be thorough; discuss all costs including tips, gratuities, delivery charges, setup charges, and taxes. Be sure of what the total cost will be and how much of a deposit you are expected to make. Find out about cancellation policies. Be sure to ask about any restrictions. If you are satisfied with the answers you're given then get a written, signed contract for whatever you rent and for any service. The contract should clearly spell out exactly what the salesperson told you. If the contract seems too basic and you have concerns, send along a letter attached to the signed contract as an amendment (see figure 9).

Figure 9: Sample Contract Amendment

Date:...
To:..
From:...

Dear (salesperson),

Thank you so much for showing me around your wonderful facility and for the time you took to go over all the details for my handfasting ceremony. I am certainly looking forward to celebrating my handfasting at your location.

The contract you have sent covers all our basic requirements. Thank you. To save you the bother of reworking the contract to cover all the specifics of our handfasting, I will consider this summarizing letter as an amendment to the contract. If the requirements listed are still acceptable to your facility, please cash the deposit check. If not, please give me a call.

As per our conversation, we also agreed on the following:

1. Our AV company will arrive at 3:30 p.m. on the day of the event to set up, and they will break down their equipment before noon on the following day.
2. Your staff will rearrange the room quickly after the ceremony (at approximately 5:45 p.m.) while the guests have hors d'oeuvres in the garden. The guests will then reenter the room for the celebration.
3- We will be using one dozen candles to light the ceremony.

Thank you again for all the time you have taken to help us organize our special day!

Sincerely,

Signature:...

Costs

The following list is based on one that is often used for traditional weddings. You may find it useful in deciding who covers which handfasting expense, should you foresee any confusion or disagreement arising.

BRIDE & FAMILY	GROOM & FAMILY
Invitations	Officiant fee, marriage-license fee
Flowers for ceremony and party	Flowers for bridal party
Ceremonial tools	Honeymoon
Gifts for bride's attendants	Gifts for groom's attendants
Bride's dress and accessories	Groom's attire
Bride's transportation to ceremony	Couple's transportation to party
Groom's ring	Bride's rings (engagement and handfasting)
Celebration meal, Cake	Celebration liquor
Music for ceremony	Music for celebration
Photography	Rehearsal dinner

Decorating

Simple equals elegant. If there is too much decoration, people will fail to notice the details. So, decide on one or two focal points. For example, at the ritual, choose the altar; at the celebration, choose the cake table. Use decoration to highlight these elements or lead the eye to them. If you are doing your own decorating, be creative, but be practical. A simple way to make the room look lovely is to adorn the walls: try small, white icicle Christmas lights and some fresh greenery; swag fabric in your special colors (tulle works well), beads (pearl, silver, gold), or cord (gold, silver, white). The possibilities are endless. Candles and torches create a warm and romantic atmosphere, but check to see when sunset occurs on your handfasting day or test the window coverings at the ceremony location to be sure that you will be able to darken the room adequately for this kind of illumination. Have lots of matches at the ready and assign a volunteer to watch over the candles.

Whatever you decide to use for decoration, think it through carefully. For example, if you want to place flowers in the corners of the room, first ask yourself: Do I need vases? Corner tables? Or a way to suspend the flowers? Will I buy bouquets or tie loose flowers together myself? With what? Do I need material or ribbon to hide the wire I use to bind the flowers? Don't forget to assemble all the decorating tools you may require — from glue guns to tables to concrete drill bits — well in advance.

If your handfasting is planned for outdoors, you will face some interesting challenges in this regard, although Nature herself will help you out with much of the decorating.

Flowers

Flowers are beautiful, meaningful, and expensive. Decide on the meaning you wish to express through flowers, as well as the look you wish to achieve, and then be creative. It isn't necessary to run up a huge florist bill when you have so many room-decorating alternatives: banners emblazoned with a family crest, strings of lights, festooned ribbon, floating candles, to name just a few. As a substitute for a costly floral bouquet, you could carry a white-leather journal with your vows inside and one red rose pinned to the cover, a favorite book of love poems, a muff, a fan, a wand, a scepter, or an herbal basket. You might even choose to carry nothing at all, instead drawing attention to your hands with gloves or gauntlets. Whether you use flowers or other types of room decoration, whether you carry a bouquet or some other keep-sake, consider not just color but also size and texture.

Doorways had great significance to the ancients. If you decide to place a wreath over the door of your handfasting venue, you can cut down on the expense by making your own rather than ordering one from a florist. There are many excellent craft books available that will provide you with thorough instructions. Alternatively, you could use a banner — perhaps one displaying family colors and initials, a symbol, or a family tartan. These are simple to make. First, decide on the look you want: a flag shape or a banner shape (which looks like a small table run-ner with a V cut out at one end and perhaps a tassel hanging from the crux of the V). Choose a family pattern, such as a tartan, or a material in one of your handfasting colors. Select an appliqué. For a banner that will hang outdoors, try to find a waterproof fabric. Consider whether the banner has to be large enough to be seen at a distance and whether you want to hang it in your home afterwards.

When you've resolved all of these considerations, draw up a list of the items you'll need to make the banner. For example: material (calcu-late a quarter-inch hem allowance); matching thread; appliqué; tassel; other decorations, such as beads or dried flowers; a glue gun; a wood or brass rod; picture wire for hanging the banner; a hammer and nails, or sticky patches if nails are not permitted.

Assemble these items and make the banner: cut the material to the size you require; hem it; fold and sew to make a casing for the rod at one end (or make casings at both ends and allow the banner to swag at the center); glue on the decorations.

Help

You will need lots of help. Decide which friends or family members to approach and let them know that you are looking for volunteers. Give them plenty of notice and afterwards send them a thank-you note or a gift; feed them well while they are addressing envelopes or sewing charms for you. But be sure that you give your volunteers tasks that they are capable of performing; for example, only assign the baking of the handfasting cake to a friend with reliable culinary skills. Note the names of your volunteers and their assignments. Follow up to see how they are doing — after all, you're the project manager!

Invitations and Thank-Yous

A handmade invitation with a few dried rose petals inserted in its envelope is lovely to receive. But if you decide to make your own handfasting invitations, be sure that you have the skill to do so and the time to make all that are required. Also, allow yourself enough time to make up a complete mailing list and address the envelopes. Your invitation message need not be as formal as that of a wedding invitation, but your guests will need to know who, when, and where for the ceremony, and when and where for the celebration. It should also convey what level of formality you are aiming for and what style of dress you expect, particularly if you are planning a theme handfasting. Include a map, if necessary; if your event is slated for outdoors, provide a rain-day card naming your alternative site. Don't forget to tell your invitees how you would like them to RSVP and include a return address.

If you are planning an event for fifty to one hundred guests — a grand, formal event — handmade invitations will be impractical, and you will have to arrange for printed ones. Browse through the wedding-invitation catalogs at a stationery store or a shopping-mall print shop. At such places you are most likely to find the best price and the greatest selection. Of course, you will need to adjust the wording on the invitation and its enclosures to suit a handfasting. When you begin to focus on the invitation enclosures for a formal celebration, the possibilities seem unlimited, but do keep the weight of each envelope in mind, otherwise you'll find yourself paying a small fortune in postage. The basic package would be the invitation itself, a response card, and a return envelope with postage.

There are a number of other items that you may decide to ask your printer to supply because you want customized printing on them. Often, a supplier will offer a discount if you purchase several products such as invitations, serviettes, and matchbooks. Some other custom-printed options include:

- A simple map (if your ceremony or celebration will be difficult to find, or you have many out-of-town guests).
- Reserved-seating card (this can be placed in the invitation envelope or set out at the celebration).
- Entrance card (this may be necessary if your handfasting is set in a public place).
- Party favors, such as matchbooks embossed with the handfasting couple's name and the date in gold.
- Programs to hand out at the ceremony that explain the handfasting.

Ask your printer to allow you the opportunity to check the proofs before the final product is printed; errors often crop up in printed material, and you want your handfasting invitations to be letter perfect.

Figure 10: A Formal Invitation and Response Card

The honor of your presence
at the handfasting of
Ms. Brigid Lassie & Mr. Bran Lad
is requested.

The couple will be united on
Saturday, the twenty-fifth of May, 2002
at four-thirty.

Please attend at The Harvest Room
22 Harvest Street, Toronto, Ontario.
Celebration to follow.

Your reply is requested by the twenty-fifth of April.

M _____

accepts _____

regrets _____

An informal invitation is your alternative to a handmade or a formal invitation. It generally takes the form of a folded card — like the typical birthday card — and requests a phoned-in or e-mailed RSVP. You can either select a blank card with a pretty decorative border and fill in the essential information yourself, or have a printer do it for you. The informal invitation works best if you are planning a smaller handfasting and celebration with people you are close to.

Figure 11: An Informal Invitation

Our dearest friends are invited to witness the handfasting of Brigid Lassie and Bran Lad.

Please be a part of this celebration of love.

WHERE
Ceremony at The Harvest Room
22 Harvest Street
Toronto, Ontario
Party to follow

WHEN
On Saturday, May 25, at four-thirty

RSVP: To Brigid at 555-5555

As you find yourself increasingly caught up in issuing invitations and planning every aspect of your special day, don't forget about thank-you notes. They are very important. You absolutely must thank everyone who sends a gift and everyone who helps you to pull your handfasting ceremony and celebration together. Keep a list of names and favors so that no one is overlooked. You may include thank-you cards in your print order, purchase them from a stationery store, or create your own.

When it comes to the gifts, it is best to stay on top of the task and send out a card as soon as you receive a gift, but, whenever you decide to do it, write a personal note that mentions the gift you were given. It only takes a sentence or two to express genuine appreciation. See figure 12 below for thank-you note samples; the second sample demonstrates that even a thank-you for a practical gift can sound warm and sincere.

Figure 12: Thank-You Notes

Dear Liz and Rob,

Bran and I were thrilled to receive the crystal decanter. We will save a bottle of wine from our handfasting, and on our first-month anniversary we will pour it into the decanter to enjoy during a romantic dinner. Thank you for your thoughtfulness.

Dear Judy and Wayne,

Thank you so much for the coffeemaker. Thanks to you, we will be able to relax on the morning after our handfasting with our favorite blend and think about how fortunate we are to have such supportive family and friends.

Location

When you decide to book a site, whether it is a restaurant, a hall, or a park, be sure to get a detailed contract, and be sure to get answers to all of your questions. Between what hours do you have the site (remember that you need time for the celebration *and* the cleanup)? Are there any restrictions (no smoking, no candles, no music)? How much is the deposit? What is the cancelation policy? Are there other rooms in the facility, making noise a concern? Are the washrooms adequate? Can you bring in chairs, food, and liquor, or do you have to purchase and/or rent these through the facility? Do you have to get a liquor license, or does the facility have one? Is there parking? Is the site easy to find? Will you need to put up direction signs for your guests?

Meals and Beverages

Food preparation and service is one of the most challenging planning tasks you will have, so make your decisions carefully. The time of day that you have chosen for your handfasting will influence the food you serve. For example, if you handfast at 5 p.m., your guests will be expecting dinner. Brunch is usually the least expensive meal; hors d'oeuvres run a close second; a buffet is usually less expensive than a sit-down meal. Your choice of which meal to serve will, in turn, dictate a host of other requirements: tables and tablecloths, servers, centerpieces, certain kitchen facilities, and so on.

If you decide to rent a venue, find out whether you are allowed to bring in your own food and liquor or your own caterer. Often, a rental facility will insist that you use its in-house caterer and bar, and this can be a far more expensive option than finding a place that allows you to bring in your own caterer and bar — unless the facility waives the rental fee in return for your use of its services. When you ask for quotes, be sure that you ask each facility for exactly the same things so that you can compare. Confirm any extra costs, such as bartender, gratuities, coat check, linen, and security.

Tied closely to meals are beverages. Are you serving liquor? Will there be special toasts? How long will it take you to get a liquor permit for your location? Do you need a bartender? Are you supplying the glasses (you will need wine, beer, and liquor glasses, and maybe even champagne flutes), the mixers, the nonalcoholic beverages? Will there be wine with the meal? Open bar or cash bar? One drinking option is to supply each guest with a drink ticket for each hour of celebration and have a cash bar for anyone who wants more.

If you elect not to hire a caterer, be prepared to take on a very big task. First, you must put someone responsible in charge. You cannot spend the day of your celebration managing the food table or manning the bar. Put one person in charge, and line up a strong team of helpers. Prior to the event this team must:

- Review, with you, the budget for food, beverages, servers, and serving supplies.
- Create the menu, with your help.
- Create the supply list. Brainstorm as a group to be sure that everything — from pickles to ice to butter knives to drinking straws — is covered. Then, for each food/beverage item, note the following:

  What container will it be transported in?
  What dish or vessel will it be served in?
  What utensils are needed to serve it?
  What utensils are needed to eat/drink it?
  How will it be kept at the right temperature?

How far in advance can it be purchased?

How will it be stored until the celebration?

Where will it be placed at the celebration?

How will it be served?

Who will serve it?

Is the item's container on loan?

Who will return the container?

Who will be responsible for any cleanup associated with it?

- Shop for food and serving supplies.
- Prepare food.
- Transport food.
- Keep food hot or cold.
- Recruit a cleanup crew for after the event.

During the event, your team must ensure that:

- Table stays attractive (clean up spills, remove lids, keep plastic wrap out of sight).
- Table is always well supplied with food.
- Table is always equipped (with forks, glasses, condiments, serviettes).
- Food remains at approximately the correct temperature.
- Individual guests' needs are seen to (someone may need a glass of water, or have a question pertaining to food allergies).

If you have opted to be your own caterer, you have probably decided on a buffet/hors d'oeuvres combination. The rule of thumb is four hors d'oeuvres per person per hour and one food station for every twenty-five guests. A food station is just a table bearing serviettes and finger food—perhaps a simple fruit-and-cheese tray or a vegetable-and-dip tray. Another party staple is Brie cheese melted in phyllo pastry, which is cut open and surrounded with bite-size pieces of French bread. Peruse party cookbooks and collect a range of recipes that appeal to you. A great way to test some of these recipes is to serve them to your hard-working volunteers as they address invitation envelopes.

Music and Entertainment

Music will enhance the mood throughout your celebration. Decide on the atmosphere you want to create, then comparison shop. If you want a live musician or a band, go to see them perform, if possible; if not, at least listen to them on tape. Friends' recommendations can be very helpful, but remember that people's tastes vary widely. An economical source for good-quality musicians—particularly classical, Celtic, or jazz—is college and university music departments. Also, your local musicians' union would be pleased to pass on the names of artists willing to audition for you via demo tape. The other option, of course, is to hire a DJ; they are typically less expensive than bands, but do try to catch the one you're considering in action to be sure that you're on the same wavelength.

If you wish to have music to complement the entire ceremony, you will need: music as the guests arrive (prelude); music as you, the hand-fasting couple, approach the altar (processional); music during parts of the ritual (ceremonial); and music as you exit as a handfasted couple (recessional). You may also want to choose songs for other special moments or circumstances during the celebration: the handfasted couple's entrance to the celebration; their first dance together; their dance with their parents; an interlude of folk dancing; the cutting of the cake; dedications and requests; a fanfare for the broom jump; the last dance before the celebration ends. Work out a detailed plan for all of this with the musicians or DJ you plan to hire.

Remember that music is not your only entertainment option. If there is an interval between the end of the handfasting ceremony and your arrival at the celebration — as the handfasted couple, you may want to detour for photographs — fill it with something inventive. What about a juggler and a bard? Or a fencing display? To arrange it, contact your local fencing club or medieval society (often within a university); or search the Internet for medieval fairs performers. If you succeed in recruiting members of the local fencing club, you might ask them to perform in character — one knight fights for the bride's family, one for the groom's. Even if you aren't charged for this, there will be some cost involved — you may be obliged to invite the performers to stay on at the celebration, or provide them with taxi fare.

Party Favors

Be sure that these are prepared well in advance. Candy, flower seeds, embossed matchbooks, incense tied with ribbon or wrapped in tulle are favorites. Use your imagination. Look at novelty items available around Valentine's Day. Check out wholesale gift suppliers on the Internet. Ask a friend to search around for you, and she may come up with everything from candles to pewter charms to chocolate hearts. The practical question is, does the volume discount on a particular party favor reduce the price enough to satisfy your budget?

Photography

Most people want their special day captured in photos or on videotape. If you want to use a professional photographer, try to get a referral from a friend. Take a look at each candidate's portfolio. Get estimates from several photographers, but choose one that can provide a level of quality that pleases you. Check with officiants and rental-location managers to be sure that photography is allowed and that there will be sufficient light. If you plan a candlelit celebration, discuss this with the photographer. Also, consider giving three friends disposable cameras. Ask them to take shots during the celebration and return the cameras to you at a later date. This way, you will have formal and informal shots of friends and family.

Repairs

If you are renting space, look around during your walkthrough to see if any repairs are needed. Ask if the facility will make these promptly. If your location is outdoors, check for a level surface to accommodate the altar and guest chairs; be sure that any trimmings, raking, or general cleaning will be taken care of. If you live in a seasonal climate, ascertain whether the site you view filled with apple blossoms in June will be as lovely in August — you may need to give nature a helping hand. If you are using a friend's home, be prepared to paint a couple of rooms, have the carpet cleaned, and wash the windows; have a cleanup crew ready to leave the home spotless after your event.

Rings

You will wear your rings for a lifetime, so be sure that you truly love the way they look. There is no need to purchase a diamond if you find yourself drawn to rubies. Buy what you like — within reason. Be aware that if you choose a ring that you can't really afford, its attractiveness will fade as the payments become burdensome. Choose a reputable jeweler, and view the ring in daylight. Make sure that your purchase agreement allows you to return the ring within a certain time period so that you can get an objective appraisal or simply change your mind. Also, check that the agreement includes sizing at no additional charge. Your jeweler's invoice should contain a thorough description of the ring so that you can insure it under your homeowner's policy.

HANDFASTING BUDGET WORKSHEET

Set up a large, columned worksheet using the headings in figure 13 below. Lay the headings out across the top of the worksheet page, as shown.

Figure 13: Budget Worksheet Headings

Task or budget item	Cost and who pays	Who arranges	Details (e.g., placement at ceremony)	Date to be completed	Check ✓ when complete

Next, make a list of tasks and related budget items and note them down the left side of the worksheet page. What follows is a suggested task and budget item list. Adapt it to suit your own special requirements.

Invitations and Thank-You Notes
- Printing/designing
- Envelopes
- RSVP card
- Notes for volunteer helpers
- Postage
- Labels
- Map
- Notes for gift givers

Photography
- Professional stills package
- Professional videotape package
- Disposable cameras for friends
- Newspaper-announcement photo

Flowers for Individuals
- Couple's parents
- Officiants
- Attendants
- Couple (e.g., bouquet, circlet for hair, boutonnieres)

Flowers for Decoration
- Ceremony
- Doorways
- Bedchamber
- Celebration
- Transportation

Couple's Attire
- Dress/suit
- Headwear
- Shoes
- Accessories (e.g., gloves, as an alternative to a bouquet)

Attendants' Attire
- Dress/suit
- Accessories (e.g., pillow for ring bearer, baskets for flower girls)
- Headwear

Handfasting Ceremony
- Location
- Music
- Other furniture or pillows
- Incense
- Salt
- Goblets
- Broom
- Charms
- Ceremonial dagger
- Repairs
- Altar
- Candles
- Oils
- Wine
- Cords
- Cauldron
- Vow book
- Guest book and pen

- Programs
- Volunteers
- Officiant (and perhaps an assistant)
- Transportation
- Cosmetic items for the couple
- Utensils or dishes for the altar items

Handfasting Celebration

- Location
- Food
- Furniture (including delivery and setup costs)
- Music
- Ceremonial cake
- Party favors
- Volunteers
- Food-service items (e.g., utensils, serving dishes, tablecloths)
- Repairs
- Beverages
- Beverage-service items (e.g., glasses, mixers, ice)
- Servers/bartenders
- Decorations
- Ceremonial cake knife
- Cleanup crew
- Toasts (e.g., list of who will toast, special glasses)

Honeymoon

- Accommodations
- Entertainment
- Passports and vaccinations
- Food
- Clothing
- Transportation from celebration

Other

- Rings
- Permits
- Rehearsal dinner
- Register for gifts
- Gifts for attendants and helpers
- Ring inscription
- License and blood tests
- Hope chest
- Rooms for out-of-town guests
- Inform volunteers of responsibilities

- Salon expenses (e.g., hair, nails)
- Emergency kit (e.g., camera, batteries, film, brush, comb, deodorant, makeup, pantyhose, mirror, a box of tissues, pen, paper, glue gun, matches, nail clippers, nail file, aspirin)

CHOREOGRAPHY

Now that you have given some thought to what you need to borrow, rent, buy, or arrange for your handfasting, you must perform one more practical task: choreography for the ceremony. You should take a quick runthrough the day before the ceremony, but months before — when you are filling in the worksheet in this chapter — you, the couple, will need to act out the handfasting. There are plenty of little things that can be overlooked if all you do is plan in your daydreams.

For example, you have decided to carry a bouquet and a vow book up to the altar and then pass these items to your maid. But how will she help with the cords if her hands are full? And, if you expect her to pass the bouquet and vow book back to you, how will you hold hands with your partner as you exit? If she keeps them, how will she pick up the broom? What if your dress has a train that you need to hold up?

But don't worry. Every problem has a solution, and if you plan early enough, that solution will be easy to find. Perhaps you could position a small table near the altar on which to set the bouquet and vow book. You could ask a friend to pick these items up after your exit and deliver them to you in time for the photo session. Allow time to arrange for the table and decide whether you want to cover or decorate it.

When you walk through the ceremony, write out stage directions for each participant, but also give each a description of the overall choreography to provide a context for his or her role. Keep the directions simple. What follows is a choreography based on the ceremony described in chapter 6, The Ceremony: Your Vows and Ritual.

- The ceremonial tools and space are organized. The ceremonial circle is created. (If these need to be purified or decorated, it is done in advance.) Just before the ceremony, an assistant helps the officiant lay out the altar and the tools.
- The guests arrive and take their seats.
- The officiant moves to the back of the altar.
- The harpist pauses.
- The officiant asks the guests to stand.
- The groomsman leads the procession.
- The couple — Brigid and Bran — approach, walking side by side.
- The maid follows, carrying the broom.
- The groomsman enters the circle and stands to the right of the altar.
- The couple enters and stands directly before the altar.
- The maid enters and stands to the left of Brigid.
- The officiant welcomes the guests.
- The maid sweeps the broom once across the circle opening and then places the broom across the opening.
- The officiant symbolically purifies the room.
- The couple steps up to the altar and each partner lights one candle.
- The officiant explains what this candle lighting means.
- The couple lights the unity candle.
- The officiant explains what the unity candle means.
- The officiant gives the blessing for the fire element.

- Brigid and Bran step back to their original places.
- The officiant gives the blessing for the air element.
- The officiant symbolically purifies the rings.
- The couple exchanges rings.
- The officiant gives the blessing for the water element.
- The couple sips the wine.
- The officiant gives the blessing for the earth element.
- The officiant announces that the vows will be exchanged.
- Brigid and Bran turn to face each other.
- Brigid speaks her personal vows.
- Bran speaks his personal vows.
- The couple turns back to the officiant.
- The officiant asks for the cords.
- The groomsman passes the cords to the officiant.
- The officiant symbolically purifies the cords.
- As the cords are being cleansed, the couple steps back far enough to allow the maid and groomsman to step up to the altar.
- The officiant hands the cords to the maid and groomsman.
- With a simple twist, the maid and groomsman shape the cords into the infinity symbol.
- The officiant asks Brigid and Bran to extend their right hands.
- They extend their right hands.
- The maid and groomsman slip the infinity loop over the couple's extended wrists.
- The officiant asks the couple to turn to each other and clasp hands.
- They turn to each other and clasp hands.
- The officiant speaks.
- Brigid and Bran answer.

- The officiant places her hand on the couple's clasped hands and speaks.
- The officiant removes her hand.
- The maid and groomsman remove the cord and place it on the altar.
- The officiant addresses the guests.
- Brigid and Bran kiss.
- The officiant speaks to the guests.
- The guests stand.
- The officiant rings the bell.
- The officiant introduces the couple.
- Brigid and Bran, hands still joined, jump the broom.
- The couple exits.
- The maid lifts the broom.
- The maid and groomsman follow the couple.
- The guests applaud then exit.
- A friend picks up any tools that need to be collected for safekeeping.

Planning your handfasting ceremony and celebration can be great fun and very inspirational. It is a time when friends and family offer their support, advice, and guidance — even those who seem a little too helpful are really just showing how much they want your handfasting day to be special. But bear in mind that it is your day, and all the decisions are yours. As a couple, make choices that reflect your shared passions. Understand the meaning of the choices you make. Choose ceremonial tools that will invite magick into your ritual. And, finally, relax and enjoy exploring the possibilities.

First rehearse your song by rote,
To each word warbling note;
Hand in hand, with fairy grace,
Will we sing, and bless this place.

—William Shakespeare, *A Midsummer Night's Dream*

Ceremonial Tools & Traditions

In the world inhabited by the ancients, the link between the spiritual and natural realms was in evidence everywhere — on land, in the sea, in the sky. It was apparent in the crashing waves of the Irish Sea that mourned the passing of the divine Dylan; in the carved cavern of the Cumae Sybil; in the protective halo-lightning lent to sailors by Castor and Pollux; and in the frigid winds of the Nordic Frost Giants. Every aspect of nature was infused with vitality and magick by the four elements: water, earth, fire, and air. And the ancients employed ceremonial tools and traditions to attract and direct these magickal energies.

Those ceremonial tools and traditions are among the most intriguing elements of handfasting. Couples who decide to use them to personalize their ceremonies soon discover that they are as varied and as rich in meaning as Nature herself. As you plan your handfasting, determine what your values are as a couple, what qualities you wish to bring to your sacred union, and then choose the ceremonial tools and traditions that will best convey these precious values and qualities to the guests at your handfasting. This chapter is comprised of an alphabetical list of these tools and traditions to assist you in your selection.

Athame

An athame is a knife or sword—usually double-edged, with a black handle—that absorbs and directs power in rituals and magick. This tool has a long tradition. Archaeologists have unearthed Celtic daggers and Viking swords, inspired by the Celtic smiths, that have runic engravings on the hilt, blade, or scabbard. King Arthur's Excalibur, of course, is the most famous of the Celtic swords.

The athame is a symbol of the masculine, the God, the sun. It represents will, passion, strength, and potency. It is sometimes identified with air, sometimes with fire—both elements of the God. In handfasting rituals, the sword is often dipped into the chalice as a symbol of the God entering the Goddess and consummating their sacred union.

Attire

In the ancient civilizations of the Mediterranean, a bride would wear a white robe to express her joy and her purity of spirit, but not necessarily her virginity. In the Far East, bright red clothing was often worn by marrying couples to symbolize love's eternal flame. Around the world and through the ages, marrying couples have chosen the style and color of clothing that holds meaning for them. Gloves, gauntlets, or bare hands have been prevailing choices in different cultures and at different moments in history. Headwear, also, has been used to reflect a couple's taste and the meaning the partners wish to convey in their union. Examples include: crowns woven of hawthorn or mistletoe twigs, wreaths of flowers and knotted ribbons, a cap or veil; if a headdress doesn't seem right, braided hair is an option.

Whether you opt for medieval attire or a simple robe, choose a color that is meaningful to you. In making your selection, consider what these colors represent:

- Red: desire, strength, and vigor
- Pink: romance, happiness, and true love
- Orange: excitement, friendship, and spontaneity
- Yellow: harmony, confidence, and creativity
- Green: nature, fertility, and good fortune
- Blue: honesty, patience, and loyalty
- Purple: friendship, insight, and power
- Brown: strength, growth, and security
- Black: strength, protection, and wisdom
- White: devotion, protection, and spiritual purity
- Silver: inspiration, optimism, and creativity
- Gold: friendship, unity, and abundance

Beltane Celebrations

Beltane rituals celebrate the union of the Goddess and the God. They are therefore a celebration of love and sensuality. To create the scene for a Beltane handfasting, a clearing is found and in it a maypole is erected; a bonfire is lit at the clearing's southernmost point. The fire symbolically cleanses the world and lights the way for lovers. The hand-fasting couple leap over the flames to burn away discord and reignite passion. Then, inspired by the divine union, the couple comes together to consummate their love. The couple approaches the maypole, which is decorated with flowers and trailing ribbons; the pole is a phallic symbol of the God inserted into the earth. Each lover chooses a ribbon and dances around the pole, laughing, singing, expressing the joy and ecstasy of the Goddess and the God. Often, the Great Rite is included in the Beltane ritual.

Broom (Besom)

The broom is an ancient symbol of purity and protection. In hand-fasting, jumping the broom represents a leap into a new life journey. Brooms were used in American slave weddings, but the roots of the practice may be traced back to the Celtic tradition. For your handfasting, choose a broom that is simply a trimmed tree branch, or buy a handmade one at a craft fair. To add special meaning to your besom, make it yourself. You will need the handle, the brush, and the cord to tie them together. Take a walk in the woods and let nature inspire you. Be guided by this list of the symbolic qualities of various woods:

- Alder: steadfast, emotional, loving
- Apple: prosperous, romantic
- Ash: compassionate, trustworthy, fair
- Birch: creative, innocent, spontaneous
- Elder: mystical, spiritual, introspective
- Hawthorn: loving, committed, fertile
- Hazel: wise, tolerant, protective
- Holly: nurturing, affectionate, idealistic
- Ivy: cooperative, loving, adoring
- Oak: powerful, confident, fertile
- Reed: understanding, principled, protective
- Rowan: expressive, protective, passionate

- Vine: joyous, lusty, prosperous
- Willow: romantic, flexible, resilient
- Yarrow: protective, steadfast, insightful

Candles

In Ancient Greece, couples were united by candlelight or torchlight. In Rome, wedding guests escorted the bride to her new hearth — a domestic temple that offered her protection. In the Celtic tradition, May Eve was celebrated with the great bonfires of Bel.

Fire, one of the four elements recognized by the ancients, is a symbol of the power that resides in creation and transformation, death and rebirth. Polarity, a driving principle of the natural world, is most evident in this element: Hephaestus's fires forged creative wonders for the gods; Hestia's hearth fire warmed the spirit and protected the home; and Zeus's gift from the Cyclops, the lightning bolt, became a symbol of rage and destruction.

The ancients used the language of astrology to describe the qualities of fire: Aries symbolized the red-hot fire, angry, volatile, and unquenchable; Leo's flame was golden and enlightening, with a brilliance that tantalized the eye and warmed the spirit; Sagittarius's fire was a mesmerizing blue flame that sparked the imagination, burning away confusion and replacing it with wisdom.

The soft glow of candlelight sets a mood. The hypnotic flicker of a flame seems alive with nature's rhythms and the power to invoke the spiritual world. Candle flames have long been used for scrying: spinning prophecies from images that manifest themselves in flame, water, or crystal.

For your handfasting, you may use candles to represent the element of fire, or, depending on their color, to symbolize other ritual elements.

If candle color is important to you, consult the list of symbolic color qualities in the "Attire" section before making your selection.

Making your own ritual candles — at least for the handfasting altar — will allow you to personalize the meaning they convey and imbue them with your energy. Mix a few drops of aromatic oil into the melted wax (or massage the oil into a store-bought candle) to enhance its spiritual qualities. Another way to add meaning is to carve runes and astrological symbols into the candle.

The simplest way to make a candle is to purchase beeswax sheets and wicks from a craft store and roll the beeswax tightly around the wick. Experiment to determine the degree of thickness that will permit the candle to burn for the amount of time that you require. Oils can be massaged into beeswax candles and symbols carved onto them. To make melted-wax candles, purchase the wax (mix paraffin and beeswax), wicks, crayons, and candle molds from your local craft store. Melt the wax gently at a low heat. Choose a crayon of an appropriate color and add it to the melting brew. If you want to scent your candles with aromatic oil, add some to the melting wax. As you work on the candle, think about your loved one and the kind of union you wish for. You may say to yourself, "As your slow flame burns let the magick release; charm our love to endure in passion and peace." Carefully pour the wax down the wicks into the molds. Let the candles cool thoroughly before unmolding.

If you plan to anoint your candles prior to the handfasting ceremony, create a blend of essential oils (see the "Oils, Massage, and Bathing" section) and sprinkle a few drops of the blend on the candle. Massage the oil into the wax in a circular fashion, using your thumbs. Work up from the center of the candle to the top, and then from the center down.

To create a spell to enhance love, assemble one rose-colored pillar candle, one rose quartz crystal, and a few drops of rose oil. With the rose quartz crystal, engrave the sign for Venus ♀ about halfway up the candle. Scratch your initials and those of your lover into the wax three times. Anoint the candle with the rose oil. During a waxing moon, burn the candle on three consecutive nights for three hours. When you first light the candle, and just before you snuff it out, guide the fragrance towards you with a wave of your hand, inhale deeply, and think of your lover.

Cauldrons

These wonderful vessels — from the cauldron of Dagda, the great Irish god and chief of the Tuatha de Danann, to the cauldrons used today for magick and ritual — have always been powerful tools of enchantment. According to ancient Celtic legend, the Goddess boiled her cauldron for a year and a day, distilling its bubbling broth into three potent drops of insight and inspiration. This magickal legend has been an inspiration to modern Witchcraft.

The cauldron is a symbol of the Goddess, the moon, the element of water, the feminine principle in nature. In the handfasting ceremony, a candle is often placed in the cauldron. The candle brings the light of the sun, the God, the primordial groom, into the body, mind, and spirit of the Goddess, the cauldron, the primeval bride. A three-legged cauldron is particularly significant, as the tripod symbolizes the Goddess in her three guises (maid, mother, and crone). As the ceremony progresses, all four elements are gathered in or around the cauldron, enclosed in the sacred space, where a magickal transformation takes place: as the lovers are joined, two become one.

Chalices

A chalice is more than a sacred cup or goblet; it is a cauldron in miniature. Just as, in Ancient Celtic tradition, Arthur's Holy Grail was a vessel of spiritual significance, so the chalice is an important symbolic tool in the handfasting ceremony. It represents the feminine, the Goddess, the moon, fertility, sensuality, and compassion. Its element is water. In handfasting rituals, the sword is often dipped into the chalice as a symbol of the God entering the Goddess and consummating their sacred union.

Charms

We can draw the energies inherent in nature together and then redirect them into an array of manifestations, just as a prism captures a ray of sunlight and bends it into a rainbow. A charm — or fetish, or amulet, or talisman — is the tool we use to do this. It is an object invested with natural power by its owner, who must believe in its ability to influence events.

Charms were used by ancient civilizations. Apollonius of Tyana, the legendary Balinas of Arabic literature, was reputed to be a "master of talismans." The Ancient Etruscans were fascinated by the magick properties of birds, animals, and trees. Like the Druids, Etruscan augurs — priests who interpreted the meaning of flight patterns and other bird behaviors — believed that the natural world was a medium for divine messages.

Druid priests practiced shapeshifting magick and animal divination. They also used charms symbolizing the energies of certain animals to enrich the handfasting ceremonies they conducted, and these charms were either sewn into hems, worn as jewelry, or pressed into candle wax. The following four animals encompass a range of symbolic possibilities, and they are the creatures most often associated with sacred unions:

- Stag: desire and potency (masculine)
- Swan: devotion and creativity (feminine)
- Hare: fertility and good fortune (feminine)
- Bull: potency and strength (masculine)

In Celtic culture, birds played an important role in magick and divination, so bird feathers were frequently used in charms and rituals. If you would like to use feathers as a ceremonial tool — as a charm, or to direct the smoke from burning incense — be sure to consider their special color symbolism and how it reflects the qualities you hope for in your union:

- White: harmony
- Yellow: friendship
- Speckled: spirituality
- Black: adaptability
- Red: prosperity
- Gray: contentment
- Brown: strength

In the medieval world, charms were always made under the proper planetary and zodiacal configurations. Talismans were fashioned on a day and at an hour when the particular celestial energies infusing the charm were at their most powerful. Go back to chapter 2, Timing: When to Handfast, and look at the figures listing the hours and days ruled by each planet to select the best moment to make your charm. For example, if you decide to pick rose petals for a love charm and sew them into the hem of your gown, wander into the garden on a Friday at sunrise, enjoy the quiet, let the heady perfume of the roses fill you with desire, and gather the petals that fall at your touch.

Take the time to ponder exactly what it is you wish to accomplish through charming.

Write out your thoughts as they develop; you may want to use a portion of this writing later, in the incantation (rhyming verse is thought to be the most potent) or the charm itself. Is loyalty and commitment uppermost in your mind? Contentment? Friendship? Passion? Your first reaction to this may be, "I want it all," but reflect on it for a little while and you may discover that you feel more secure in some areas than in others. Concentrate the power of the charm where it is most needed. Remember that you can always create more than one charm.

You may pin or sew your charms inside the hem of your handfasting attire or the altar cloth. Alternatively, press them into a book of verse or tuck them into the satchel that will hold your vows during the ceremony. A pretty charm can be tied into the flower arrangement with a ribbon, added to a centerpiece, used as a decoration at the base of a candle, or tucked into a pocket to be stroked for good luck during the special day.

A fragrant charm can remind you of its potency while gently scenting your handfasting attire. Place the charm in your closet, in your lingerie drawer, even under your mattress. Or tuck it into the toe of your shoe —

shoes have long been a symbol of entering into a new life (if your charmed shoes have laces, make a wish as you knot them).

Charming is an intimate undertaking. It compels you to summon the power of your emotions and invest that power in the object or material you have chosen. Charming can be as simple as holding a rose quartz to your heart while meditating on your lover's being; it can also be a ritual that invokes the energies of the natural world to assist you. For example, a charm to deepen love consists of: one pink candle, one white candle, a circle of soft pink cloth, a pinch of soil, one apple seed, three drops of lavender oil, a sprig of rosemary and a twelve-inch blue ribbon. Prepare your charm on a Monday at sunset during a waxing moon by the light of the two candles — pink for love, white for purity. Lay out the pink cloth. Place the pinch of earth at the center of the circle as a symbol of the strong foundations of your love. Set the apple seed on the soil. Sprinkle the lavender oil on the seed for happiness. Place a few leaves of the rosemary — for memories of friendship and intimacy — in your hand, and gently blow these onto the cloth. Gather the edges of the cloth together, making a pouch. Wrap the blue ribbon — for loyalty and respect — around the pouch three times. Set the pouch between the lights of the two candles and tie three knots. As you tie each knot, say, "We will reap what we sow, let our true love bond deepen and grow."

Handmade charms are receptacles for the personal power of the individual who creates them, but charms that are crafted by others and charms that are chanced upon in their natural state have an impressive potency of their own. There are myriad talismans for you to choose from. Traditionally, feathers, metal, or crystals were used. In antiquity, wands, scepters, and crowns were encrusted with crystals and gems because (beauty and status aside) they focused power and afforded their bearer a charmed protection. Charms created by metalsmiths in the images of powerful animals or symbols were also considered highly effective talismans. In Ancient Egypt, one popular talisman was a heart wrought of copper — Venus's metal — or carved from red stones like jasper, cornelian, bloodstone, ruby, and garnet, or formed from red glass or wax. To the Celts, the acorn, fruit of the sacred oak tree, was a talismanic symbol of longevity; and the shamrock was a representation of the three guises of the Goddess that offered protection and prosperity.

In the medieval world, the horse symbolized protection and good fortune. Horseshoes, which became enduring tokens of good luck, were often fastened above the doorways of ceremonial spaces. More recently, in the Victorian era, charms of silver and gold were exchanged by lovers. Each represented a special promise:

- Cat: good luck
- Coin: wealth and prosperity
- Heart: romantic love
- Horseshoe: a fortunate future
- Knot: loyalty in love
- Wishbone: a wish to come true

When you have decided on the purpose of your charm and selected an appropriate object of material for it, perform an incantation, or simply hold the charm to your heart, allowing the magick of your spirit — of your heart chakra, of your personal power — to penetrate it. You have now put the charm to work making your ultimate wish come true. Before you consign your charm to a special place, you may consider knotting it into a circle of cloth of a color that will help direct the charm's energy. Use this list of color symbols to choose the right hue:

- White: to ensure protection
- Black: to hear the truth
- Silver: to enhance imagination and creativity
- Blue: to increase loyalty and mend a broken heart
- Brown: to build a strong friendship
- Green: to attract income or money

- Orange: to bring happiness
- Yellow: to encourage confidence
- Pink: to bring romance
- Purple: to increase psychic ability and foster deeper spiritual understanding
- Red: to enhance passion
- Gold: to find hope and optimism

Cords

The custom of demonstrating a couple's commitment through ceremonial binding is an ancient one. In Assyria, the groom's father would tie the hands of the bride and groom together with a strand of wool. The Sumerians pulled a thread from the garment of each and used the threads to join them to one another. The Brahmans used a red cloth to bind marrying couples. In Thailand, a Brahman rope is still used for that symbolic purpose. Sir Walter Scott portrayed handfasting ceremonies as common occurrences in Scotland of the 1700s. And modern-day Druids continue to practice the knotted-cord handfasting ritual.

The cords used during the handfasting ceremony are an apt symbol of the commitment that the lovers have chosen to make. When the cords are removed, the will, the intent, and the oath the couple shares continue to hold them fast. The bond remains as long as love endures and the couple chooses to maintain their commitment.

In the Celtic tradition, the cord is the symbol and the knot is the magickal element. The tying of the knot is the making of a wish. That is why the handfasting partners must prepare the cords themselves. To prepare your handfasting cord, you will need: two lengths of cord (of a type that will hold knots), each two feet long; several ribbons of significant colors; and one white satin bag. Choose a quiet, relaxed time to make your preparations. If you wish to purify the cord, one way of doing it is by passing it through the smoke of sage incense. When this is done, the man grasps the lengths of cord in either hand while the woman ties a knot, attaching the cords to form a single length. As she does so, she fills her mind and heart with loving thoughts, and if she has a wish, she thinks of it—or, better yet, says it aloud. Next, she holds the cord while her partner ties his knot with the loose ends of the cord, forming a circle.

At some point before the handfasting, use the cord to practice making an infinity symbol with your maid and groomsman. The moment when they use it to bind the hands of you and your partner will be the focal point of your ceremony, and you'll want it to unfold smoothly. The infinity symbol is a loose, sideways number 8. It is simple to create: The maid takes one side of the knotted cord, the groomsman the other. Together they hold the cord so that it forms an elongated O. The maid then turns the cord once, twisting it into the figure 8. It is now ready for the attendants to set over the wrists of the handfasting couple.

If you would like to empower your cord with even more wishes, then tie the symbolically colored ribbons along it. Choose cord and ribbon colors that symbolize your hopes, using this list to guide your selection. Each of these colors represents a wish:

- White: true love, devotion, and protection
- Black: adaptability, companionship, and protection
- Silver: imaginativeness, optimism, and patience
- Blue: honesty, peacefulness, and devotion
- Brown: balance, security, and strength
- Green: abundance, luck, and potential
- Orange: excitement, spontaneity, and friendship
- Yellow: confidence, creativity, and delight

- Pink: romance, passion, and happiness
- Purple: spirituality, insight, and companionship
- Red: desire, potency, and strong emotion
- Gold: friendship and prosperity

Crystals, Gemstones, and Rings

Nature's gems have always been cherished, whether they were considered to be star splinters showered on the earth by Apollo, or gifts from Gaia's molten depths, or treasures from the realm of Poseidon gift-wrapped in oyster shells. All cultures have marveled at the power of crystals to heal and protect, as well as at their power to energize the most sacred of rituals and initiations.

Light, the physical world's highest form of energy, is manipulated within the depths of each crystal prism. Throughout history, people have understood that crystals radiate and transmit great amounts of power. When they are used in charms, they are capable of summoning the forces of nature and warding off evil. Pendulum divination and crystal scrying are practices that exploit a crystal's ability to channel or penetrate other dimensions and levels of consciousness. Different crystals vibrate at different frequencies. These vibrations draw an individual to one crystal instead of another by harmonizing with that person's emotional frequency.

When choosing a crystal or gemstone as a love token or for your rings, allow yourself to be entranced by its beauty, understand its meaning in nature's design (see figure 14, page 92), and let it radiate the love you offer. To choose a crystal, first fill your heart and mind with impressions of your lover. Then handle various gemstones and crystals until one distinguishes itself; remember that a crystal held in the right hand transmits energy, while a crystal held in the left hand receives it. Try pink tourmaline (heart chakra/Venus)—it makes an ideal love token, since it inspires trust in the power of love and in the joy of sharing.

Figure 14: Crystals and Gemstones

GEMSTONE	MEANING	ELEMENT/CHAKRA	ASSOCIATION
Amber	compassion	air/2nd	God
Amethyst	spirituality and contentment	water/6th	Goddess
Aquamarine	optimism and joy	water/5th	Goddess
Aventurine	wealth	air/4th	God
Azurite	spiritual insight	fire/6th	God
Bloodstone	physical well being	fire/1st	God
Citrine	abundance	fire/3rd	God
Cornelian	love (from Latin for heart)	earth/2nd	Goddess
Emerald	happiness	earth/4th	Goddess
Diamond	purity and peace	fire/7th	God
Garnet	true friendship	earth/1st	Goddess
Lapis lazuli	divine inspiration	air/6th	God
Malachite	truth	earth/4th	Goddess
Moonstone	good fortune	water/4th	Goddess
Obsidian	power	fire/1st	God
Peridot	empathy and sincerity	earth/4th	Goddess
Pink tourmaline	protection and love	air/4th	God
Rose quartz	nurturing and affection	water/4th	Goddess
Ruby	true love and passion	fire/2nd	God
Sapphire	fidelity and good luck	air/6th	God

Topaz	prosperity	air/3rd	God
Turquoise	harmony	air/5th	God

Once you have chosen the stone, cleanse it. A simple way to clear the negative energy from a crystal is to place it in sunlight until it is hot to the touch. A more thorough cleansing process (for crystals that won't be damaged by salt) is to let the crystal sit submerged in a bowl of water and sea salt for three days; afterwards, place it in the sunlight for three hours.

When you have cleansed the crystal, fill it with your personal energy. While it still holds the warmth of the sun, hold it in your right hand. Focus your thoughts on your lover. Imagine the energy flowing from your heart, down your arm, out from your palm, and into the crystal. Fold the crystal into a white cloth until you are ready to present it to your lover. The crystal can be made into a ring, a pendant, or a charm, or it can be set in a special place in your home. Remember to cleanse it again from time to time.

For your handfasting, you will most likely decide to partake of a long tradition and include rings in the ritual. Before the ceremony, don't forget to follow these steps: hold the rings in your right hand; clasp them to your heart; concentrate on your love; then wrap the rings in a white cloth.

These rings you are empowering will probably be crafted from precious metals and gems, but the earliest wedding rings were bands of braided reed or strips of leather. Later, when metals became popular, the wedding ring took on a practical symbolism: it came to represent the bride's price and a husband's pledge to share his wealth. A Roman bride would often be presented with two rings — a key ring made of iron that held the keys to the pantry (a symbol of her husband's trust and sharing), and a delicate piece of jewelry to wear on formal occasions. But the ring has always been a romantic symbol, as well. The ancient Egyptians believed that in the fourth finger of the left hand was a vein that ran to the heart. The Egyptian hieroglyphic symbol for eternity is the circle; so, the ring worn on the fourth finger of the left hand represented eternal love.

The circle is a magickal symbol in its own right. It is perfect, and in its perfection it is a magickal tool for good and a form of protection against evil. Because it has no beginning and no end, it symbolizes eternity and infinity. It is the promise shared by two lovers for perfect, unending love.

At different points in history, people have worn rings on every finger, including the thumb, and on both hands. Styles and designs have changed over time. Some old English rings featured two clasped hands, symbolizing a perfect fit. These were inspired by the Roman fede (or faith) rings of a similar design. Variations on the clasped-hands motif were two hearts joined with a key or a pair of hands cupping a stone — such as a garnet, which represents the heart and love. The Ancient Celts designed rings with intricate knot patterns, the knot being yet another magickal symbol for the binding together of two lives, two souls, two lovers.

During the Elizabethan era, the gimmal (from the Latin word for *twin*) wedding ring was very popular. It consisted of two or three separate rings whose patterns interlocked, and many were based on the Celtic love-knot design. During the engagement period, the bride wore one ring, the groom wore another, and a witness wore a third. The circle's protective powers would shield the couple's love until the wedding ceremony, at which point the three rings would be combined into one and placed on the bride's finger.

In the Victorian era, expressions of love or lover's names were spelled out on betrothal and wedding rings with gems whose names began with the appropriate letters. For example, a bride named Sara would be given

a ring bearing her name spelled out in sapphires, aquamarines, rubies, and amethysts. The sentiment "adored" would be spelled out in amethysts, diamonds, opals, rubies, epidotes, and diamonds. (There is a semiprecious gem or crystal for every letter of the alphabet.)

The earliest engraved rings were found in Egyptian tombs. In the 1300s, betrothal rings — or "posy" rings — were inscribed on their outer surfaces. Ring inscriptions, which later became more common on the ring's inner surface, have often consisted of rhymes, but any loving thought is considered appropriate. If you are thinking about an inscribed ring for your handfasting, here's one variation on the custom that you might like to consider: ask that the inscription — perhaps the date and your names — be done across two rings, so that they must be placed together for the inscription to be complete.

The last major innovation in wedding and engagement ring design was made in the late 1800s, by Tiffany, the renowned jeweler. The diamond solitaire enjoyed immediate popularity, because it allowed light to pass under the stone, causing it to sparkle brilliantly.

As you can see, you have a wealth of tradition to fall back on in selecting rings for your handfasting. Perhaps, like so many couples today, you'll decide to design your own rings and commission a jeweler to make them for you. Because the modern family has evolved, taking on a more flexible structure, your handfasting may involve children from previous unions, and, in designing your own rings, you can include them in the ritual. The rings will thus symbolize the new family, not just the handfasting couple. There are several ways to design rings for this purpose: use a Celtic knot design with a separate thread for each member of the family; mount the birthstones (see figure 15, page 96) of each child on the rings; or have individual rings made for each child.

Figure 15: Birthstones

MONTH	BIRTHSTONE	MEANING
January	garnet	true friendship
February	amethyst	honesty and contentment
March	aquamarine	optimism and joy
April	diamond	purity and peace
May	emerald	happiness
June	pearl	protection
July	ruby	true love and passion
August	peridot	empathy and sincerity
September	sapphire	fidelity and good luck
October	opal*	good fortune
November	topaz	prosperity
December	turquoise	contentment

*Only in the last century have opals been labeled a stone of ill fortune, perhaps because they were so fragile jewelers became reluctant to work with them.

Once you've chosen the design of your handfasting rings and the stones that will adorn them, you must decide which metal to use. The Egyptians favored gold, as it represented the sun and creation. Silver, which was in use as early as 2,400 B.C.E., has always been associated with the moon; it is said that if you make a wish while holding a silver coin in such a way that it reflects the moon's glow, then your wish will come true. Brass, a blend of copper and zinc, was long believed to hold the power to purify and protect. In Ancient Rome, copper was thought to be the metal of love. This is because the goddess of love, Venus, rose from the sea by the island of Cyprus, and, in antiquity, Cyprus had abun-dant copper resources. Select the metal that best complements the ring design and gem you have settled on, bearing in mind the metal's histor-ical symbolism and magickal properties.

Food and Drink

The union of a loving couple has always been celebrated with a feast. Food is more than a symbol; it is a gift from the gods. The harvest, nature's bounty, is a manifestation of the divine; the feast is an opportunity to commune with the God and the Goddess. As such, the practice has been sacred since ancient times. Its power to bring people together — body, mind, and soul — should not be underestimated.

The tradition of tossing a piece of the handfasting cake evolved from a Roman wedding custom: the bride would share a morsel of biscuit with the groom and then the two would toss the crumbs onto the bride's head as a wish for fertility and abundance. Today, in Scotland, a piece of cake is still tossed over the bride's head as a wish for prosperity, and at Macedonian weddings, a loaf of bread is broken over the bride's head as a wish for fertility.

Another popular handfasting tradition is for guests to throw food at the couple when the ceremony is complete. (Raw rice was once a popu-lar tossing item until people realized that it was killing the birds that ate the leftovers.) The ceremonial throwing of food has two traditional meanings: it signifies the hope that a given union will be as successful and abundant as the harvest; and it is a means of warding off evil spirits. One modern variation on the food-tossing custom is to blow bubbles at the handfasting couple. While this looks lovely, it dilutes the signifi-cance of the action. By throwing food, handfasting guests are blessing the couple with the fruits of the earth — birdseed or breadcrumbs are a much more meaningful choice than bubbles.

Certain foods have special symbolism, and even some magickal properties. There are many ways to incorporate such foods into your handfasting feast. You can add small quantities to the handfasting cake, employ them in the ceremony itself, or use them in charms. When you cook with these foods, have fun and be positive; your emotions will increase their vibrations. Just think of your personal energy as another ingredient! Here is a list of foods that are easily added to recipes and the qualities they symbolize:

- Ale: prosperity
- Almond: protection and prosperity
- Apple: romantic love and abundance
- Banana: prosperity
- Bread/wheat: fertility and prosperity
- Caraway seeds: loyalty and dependability
- Cherry: desire
- Chocolate: passion
- Cinnamon: vitality
- Coconut: trust
- Egg: fertility
- Ginger: invigoration
- Hazelnut: wisdom
- Honey: fertility and sweet love
- Lemon: fidelity
- Orange: faithfulness and fertility

- Peppermint: seduction
- Poppy seeds: good fortune
- Rosemary: remembrance
- Sesame seeds: fertility
- Strawberry: sensuality
- Vanilla: passion
- Walnut: protection

The handfasting cake is a very special symbol. In the 1800s, finely milled flour became widely available, leavening agents like baking powder were invented, and lighter, more delicate cakes became popular; prior to that, heavy fruitcakes and (earlier still) biscuits or buns were served at wedding feasts. These sweet offerings were baked full of meaning. Some ingredients would be sweet, others bitter to symbolize a couple's ability to survive the good times as well as the bad. Fruits generally represented fertility; nuts stood for prosperity. The handfasting lovers feed one another pieces of the cake — light or fruit-and-nut laden — and this constitutes their symbolic first meal together.

When the time comes for you to choose what type of handfasting cake to serve to your guests, consider, yet again, the meanings you want to convey with your ritual. Use traditional ingredients with powerful qualities, and select icing or decoration colors that express your special wishes. If, however, you would prefer to avoid the complications and the expense of a highly decorated cake, or if many of your guests do not like fruitcake, think about serving a sweet bread, instead. A braided loaf can be a meaningful, aromatic, and delicious alternative. Round out your simple dessert course with fruit, sherbet, or ice cream.

The following sweet-bread recipe serves about ten people.

BRAIDED LOAF

Ingredients

- 1 tsp. white sugar
- 2 tbsp. active dry yeast
- 2 tbsp. butter
- 1 whole egg
- pinch of spice (e.g., cinnamon)
- 1/2 cup wheat germ
- 1/4 cup seeds or dried fruit
- 1 tbsp. sesame seeds
  (or other seeds)

- 1 cup warm water
- 3 tbsp. honey
- 1 tsp. salt
- 1 separated egg
- 1/2 cup whole-wheat flour
- 2 cups white, all-purpose flour
- 1 1/2 tsp. water

Method:

1. Dissolve sugar in warm water in a large bowl. Sprinkle yeast over water surface. Let stand fifteen minutes. Grease another large bowl and set aside.

2. Add honey, butter, salt, whole egg, 1 egg yolk, pinch of spice, whole-wheat flour, wheat germ, and 1 cup of the white flour to the yeast mixture. Using an electric mixer, beat on high for three minutes, slowly adding the remaining cup of white flour. Knead dough for ten minutes, then place in the greased bowl. Roll the dough around the bowl until it is coated in oil. Cover bowl, and allow dough to rise in a warm place for one hour (or until it doubles in size).

3. Punch dough down. Knead in dried fruit or seeds (a few rose petals may even be added at this point). Roll the dough into three,

long (12-inch) strands. Place the strands side-by-side on a greased cookie sheet. Braid loosely. (You can leave the braid long, or curl it into a circular wreath shape.) Pinch the ends together to finish neatly. Beat egg white with water, and brush onto braid. Sprinkle with sesame seeds. Let the loaf rise in a warm place for one hour.

4. Bake in a 350-degree oven for 30 minutes. Cool on a rack.

Since the days of the Greeks and Etruscans, wine has symbolized fertility, as well as prosperity and abundance. At your handfasting, you may want to share a ceremonial drink with your partner as you seal your bond by sharing a meal. You'll need a special brew for a special moment, when the clink of glasses mimics the tinkle of the bell that wards off evil and summons the faery folk to join in the celebrations. If you want to enter that deeply into Celtic tradition, you may choose to serve meade or mulled wine. Experiment with the recipes that follow — especially the meade — until you achieve a degree of sweetness that suits your palate. And be sure to serve these beverages fresh — they don't age well.

MEADE
Ingredients

- 3 cups water
- 1/4 tsp. cinnamon
- 1 bottle dry white wine
- 1/4 cup lemon juice
- 2 cups honey, or to taste

Method:

Bring 2 cups of water to a boil. Add lemon juice, cinnamon, and honey. Boil for five minutes, stirring frequently. Skim off any film that has formed on the surface and strain the mixture into a clean pot. Add white wine. Drink warm or cool. Makes 8 cups.

MULLED WINE
Ingredients

- 1 tsp. cloves
- 1 tsp. nutmeg
- 1 cup orange juice
- 1 lemon, sliced
- 1 tbsp. gingerroot, peeled and sliced
- 4 cinnamon sticks
- 1/2 cup water
- 1 cup honey or brown sugar
- 1 bottle dry red wine

Method:

Wrap in cheesecloth: cloves, cinnamon sticks, gingerroot, and nutmeg. In a pot, simmer gently (do not allow to boil) for one hour, stirring occasionally: water, orange juice, honey or brown sugar, lemon, red wine, and the cheesecloth sack. Remove spice sack and serve warm. Makes 8 cups.

It is a wonderful experience to cook with nature's bounty. Play with the aromas of various spices and the textures of different fruits and grains. The rich fragrance of mulled wine will awaken primal memories of hearth and home and bring on warm feelings of anticipation as you approach the time of your sacred union.

Great Rite

Sumerian texts from the third millennium B.C.E. tell of the union of the great goddess Inanna and her lover, Dumu-zi. Their story is mirrored in the unions of many ancient goddesses and gods, including the Goddess and the Horned God of modern Wicca.

So deeply did Inanna mourn the late-autumn death of Dumu-zi, god of corn and grains, that she followed him into the underworld, leaving the upperworld barren. By springtime, she had rescued Dumu-zi, and their renewed passion reinvigorated the world. The Goddess, the Earth Mother, the womb, accepts the seed of the Grain God so that Nature will see all of her plants and animals reborn. Through the summer, the Goddess and the God nurture the growth, and in late summer the harvest is reaped. By autumn, the God is again feeling the pull of death, and so the cycle continues. But this is not a tale of death: the God's death is, in fact, a passage to a mystical realm, a stage in the preparation for rebirth. This is a story of life, renewal, fertility, and prosperity.

In ancient cultures, the reunion of the Goddess and the God was celebrated each spring in a sacred ceremony. In particular, the annual ceremony honoring the divine union was enacted as a sacred rite by the ruler and the high priestess of Sumer as a means of ensuring fertility, prosperity, and peace for the coming year.

In modern-day Beltane celebrations, lovemaking and the magickal transformation that it gives rise to are honored. On Beltane, couples dance around bonfires and then rush off to the fields to act on the Goddess's creed — "All acts of love and pleasure are my rituals." The Pagan world is a sensual world, a divine world in every respect. To be sensual, to give pleasure to another and receive it in return, is to partake of the magick.

In the Pagan worldview, fertility and procreation are revered. Human sensuality and sexuality are simply their expressions. The Great Rite is a ritual that honors these creative energies. If you plan to include the Great Rite in your handfasting, there are different ways you can do it. Some people use the ceremonial insertion of the God's athame into the Goddess's chalice to represent the sacred marriage. Others practice an enactment, either actual or symbolic, of the consummation of the sacred marriage: a high priestess and a high priest invoke the spirits of the Goddess and the God—symbols of the polarities in nature that join to create life itself—and then they, themselves, unite.

If you decide not to have the Great Rite as a part of your handfasting ceremony, you may still call upon the Goddess and the God in any one of their various partnered guises, for example:

- Anat and Baal (Canaanite)
- Aphrodite and Adonis (Greek)
- Boann and Dagda (Celt)
- Freyja and Freyjr (Norse)
- Inanna and Dumu-zi (Sumerian)
- Ishtar and Tammuz (Babylonian)
- Isis and Osirius (Egyptian)
- Psyche and Cupid (Roman)

Incense

Your handfasting ceremony should be a sensual experience for all in attendance. That is, the qualities of your sacred union should be communicated through all the senses. Use incense to send fragrant scents, alive with meaning, wafting through the air. The incense can be lit in a censer, or some other safe type of burner. Many people use a smudge stick—a bundle of herbs or incense—to purify the sacred space. Incense can represent air and/or fire. Here is a list of incenses and what they represent to help you with your selection:

- Apple: love and fertility
- Basil: protection and patience
- Cedar: purity and prosperity

- Cinnamon: stimulation and sensuality
- Cloves: spirituality and devotion
- Frankincense: love and protection
- Heather: optimism and good fortune
- Jasmine: sensuality and insight
- Lavender: happiness and contentment
- Marjoram: joy and anticipation
- Rose: love and affection
- Rosemary: remembrance and tolerance
- Sage: cleansing and protectiveness
- Sandalwood: sexuality and desire
- Vanilla: passion and sensuality

Love Knots and Spells

In Northern Europe, knots have long been a symbol of trust, commitment, and undying love. But do not confuse the Celtic knot with a simple twist of yarn. Take a look at *The Book of the Kells*, or the glorious illuminated manuscripts of the Middle Ages for fine examples of intricate Celtic knot work.

Knots hold magic. In a custom associated with Druid handfasting and Beltane rituals, the lovers tie loose knots of ribbon onto branches of a mature oak tree. Every knot they tie is a wish. If, when the wind blows, the knots become unfastened, their wishes will be granted. So, a knot is a wish, and a wish is a spell. A handfasting, itself, is a very powerful spell in this sense — a wish for enduring love, fertility, prosperity.

But, beyond the overarching wish of the handfasting ceremony itself, there are a number of small, simple wishes that a couple can make to add fun and romance to their union. Think of it this way: magick comes from using your personal energy to influence outcomes. When you give a red rose to a special person and ask that person for a date, you must believe that your wish for a positive response will come true. If you doubt it, you will feel compelled to control and manipulate the situation, thereby blocking the natural flow of energy. When you cast a spell, you must accept what follows — in the end, it will be what your heart most needs. It is essential that you keep this in mind when you are devising your handfasting spells; take time to work out what it is you really want to accomplish, and then allow it to happen.

For a handfasting, you'll likely want to cast a love spell. To do this successfully, your heart has to be full of loving feelings. If you are angry, or even lustful, the spell will carry those energies, instead. Ideally, you are feeling contented, and you have a sense of anticipation. But don't cast the spell when you're anxious or obsessed. Remember always that your emotions are the energizing force. Before casting your spell, give yourself some time to relax, or perhaps meditate. If you wish to create a protective circle to raise natural energies to assist you in your spell casting, refer to chapter 5, Sacred Space and Divination.

Cast your spell when the moon is waxing, so that your love may grow and come to its full brilliance in harmony with the forces of nature. In chapter 2, Timing: When to Handfast, look at figures 4 (page 37) and 7 (page 44) to determine the optimum time to act. The planets best suited for love spells are the moon, Venus, and Jupiter. And in some spells, when sex is the object, or when a man is trying to attract a woman, an hour and day dominated by Mars is most advantageous.

The words of your spell should be plain and heartfelt. Don't worry if you veer from the script; the most important thing is that you say what you feel. Be sure that you understand each step in the ritual. If you know the purpose of each element, you will be able to speak from the heart consistently. Should you reach a point where you run out of words, just pause and imagine the person you love — words are only one means of projecting what we think and feel. Here is a simple love-enhancing spell that you may want to use to enrich your handfasting. For it, you'll need: two pink roses (earth); two small glasses of white grape juice or champagne (water); one empty wine glass; one white candle (fire); one rose-colored candle; lavender oil (air); rose oil; and a white cloth. Set aside a Friday evening during a waxing moon for your spell casting. At about 8 p.m., lay your tools out on a table. Put a few drops of the lavender oil on the white candle and massage it into the wax. Prepare a warm bath scented with a few drops of the rose oil. Place the rose-colored candle by the tub and light it. Soak in the tub until you feel relaxed and cleansed, then enter the room where you have laid out your tools.

You are now ready to cast the spell. Sit down, and slowly allow your feelings of love to surface; they are the energy that makes the magick work. Try to keep those feelings in your heart. From time to time, imagine your lover. Light the white candle, saying, "Let our love be a light that glows ever bright." Keep sitting quietly and comfortably. Breathe deeply. As you breathe in, imagine the light from the white candle coming towards you and surrounding you with its peaceful, golden glow. As you breathe out, imagine your doubts and worries being blown out of your thoughts, out of your life, and right out the door of the house you are in. When you feel content, open your eyes and continue.

Pick one of the roses and inhale its scent deeply. Exhale. Say, "My heart holds love deep and true. Let our love grow strong, ever fresh and new." Allow thoughts of your lover to stir your heart. Pour the two glasses of juice or wine into the empty glass. Pull a petal from the rose and drop it into the liquid, saying, "Let our fates flow along, ever side by side, bound together as one with love as our guide." Spread out the white cloth. Dip the fourth finger of your left hand into the glass, and let a drop fall from your finger onto the cloth. Pull another petal from the rose and blow on it. Set it on the cloth. Gather together the corners of the cloth, forming a small sack. Pass the sack over the candle flame, saying, "The power of Nature is gathered here. Let her nurture this love that we hold so dear." Continue with, "Let the element of fire bring us passion and desire. Let water's sensual potion stir feeling and devotion. In earth be found love's solid ground. Let the element of air grant us dreams to share."

Again, take a moment to sit quietly, eyes closed, breathing deeply, thinking of your lover. Snuff — rather than blow — out the white candle. Because the energy you've invoked will not immediately dissipate, engage in a related activity until it does, rather than forcing the energy to dissolve by introducing a negative activity. Write a love letter or a note to a good friend, read a sentimental book, or look through photo albums until you feel the energy focus shift. (You may even choose this moment to sketch out your handfasting vows.)

For a simple spell to enhance passion — which you may conduct with your partner or, if necessary, a likeness of your partner — you will need: a sprig of rosemary (earth); a goblet of water (water); one deep-red candle (fire); jasmine or ylang-ylang oil (air); and a decorative dagger or letter opener. Set aside a Tuesday evening during a waxing moon to cast this spell. At about 10 p.m., lay your tools out on a mat on the floor. Massage a few drops of jasmine oil into the wax around the wick of the red candle. Prepare a warm bath scented with a few drops of the oil. Place the red candle by the tub and light it. Drop a few leaves of the rosemary into the tub. Soak in the tub until you feel relaxed and cleansed, then bring the candle into the room where you have laid out the tools.

You are now ready to cast the spell. Sit quietly for a few moments, holding your lover's hand (or looking at his or her likeness) and thinking of the time you have spent together. Feel the love you share. Relight the red candle (if necessary), saying, "Out of darkness comes the light. Let the fires of our passion begin to ignite." Sprinkle a few drops of the oil onto the candle. As the smoke rises, say, "With each breath we draw in, let love's desire slowly begin." Keep sitting quietly and comfortably. Breathe deeply. Imagine the glow of the candle as a warmth that is beginning to envelop you. Think of your lover. When you feel content, continue.

Dip the fourth finger of your left hand into the goblet, and let a drop of water fall from your finger onto your lover's tongue. Take the spring of rosemary and blow it towards your lover. Say, "Let my love long remember the touch of me, and want and yearn for intimacy." Dip the dagger into the goblet and say, "The power of Nature is gathered here. Air, earth, fire, and water do appear as sacred elements that fan and fire, our burning love and aching desire."

Again, take a moment to sit quietly, eyes closed, breathing deeply. Imagine the golden light around you and your lover. Imagine being pulled into a warm embrace. When you feel a longing so strong that you want to open your eyes to reach out to your lover, the spell is cast. Snuff—rather than blow—out the candle. As the spell's energy gradually dissipates, go with its natural flow. If your lover is with you, let your feelings lead you. If you are casting the spell alone, go outside. While your passionate nature is still charged, send your energies out into the natural world: wish on a star, search out the planet Venus, listen to the sounds of the night.

Music and Maypole

The Greek sage Pythagoras believed that the secrets of the natural world could be unlocked through an understanding of music and mathematics. He was convinced that the planets vibrated in different, yet harmonious tones — the music of the spheres was the music of life itself. The ancients revered this music, perceiving it as the chanting of the gods. They thought that it protected against evil and offered a way for humanity to unite with the divine. Such beliefs became part of the handfasting ceremony; a bell was one of the instruments used to symbolize the music of life during the ceremony. The maypole ritual and various ceremonial dances included in the ceremony are also closely tied to the notion of divine music.

The maypole is an ancient fertility symbol. May Day celebrations in the medieval villages often took the maypole as their focal point. Village youths would rise at dawn and head out into the fields and forests to gather greenery and flowers to decorate the pole with the Goddess's finery. The pole itself is a phallic symbol, representing the masculine, the God. It is pushed into the earth, the feminine, the Goddess, as a means of celebrating the sacred union and the prosperity that it will bring to the community.

Long, streaming ribbons, raised by spring breezes, entice couples to dance around the maypole. From the Dionysian rituals to the dances of the Mevlevi dervishes to the first dance of the handfasting couple, spiraling music and dance have always invited believers to commune with the divine and unite with the energies of nature.

Oils, Massage, and Bathing

Essential oils are extracted from trees, plants, flowers, and herbs. How and why they act on the body, mind, and soul is a complex question. Research shows that the chemical components of these oils interact with body chemistry in a gentle manner. Specific oils have an affinity with specific body parts or systems. And when an oil is released, it is thought to signal the body's response to the substance's healing properties. It can take up to two hours for an oil to be fully absorbed into the body, and several more hours for its residue to be expelled. Blending oils does more than enhance fragrance; it compounds their various properties.

Oils are used in the handfasting ceremony, but there are many other ways to enjoy them: use them to purify your bath or to set a mood with their special aromas; wear them as perfumes or massage with them. A lovely ritual that may aid you, the handfasting couple, in learning about each other's touch preferences is to mix a special blend of oils and then anoint one another with it for the three nights prior to your handfasting. Continue this ritual on the new moons of your love. The following is a list of essential oils and their properties that will assist you in creating your personal blend for your handfasting or lovers' ritual.

- Basil: tolerance
- Carnation: affection
- Cedar*: abundance
- Chamomile: relaxation
- Cinnamon: stimulation
- Cloves*: devotion
- Frankincense: soothing
- Gardenia: harmony
- Geranium: protection
- Jasmine*: faithfulness
- Lavender*: contentment
- Marjoram: optimism

- Musk: sexuality and stamina
- Orange: energy
- Orange blossom: fertility
- Patchouli*: anticipation
- Rose*: heart warming
- Rosemary: remembrance
- Sage: purification
- Sandalwood*: desire
- Vanilla*: passion and sensuality
- Yarrow: romantic love
- Ylang-ylang*: passion

*Aphrodisiacs: certain plants have been used since antiquity in love spells and charms. They exude an erotic scent, and many people have speculated that this is because they mimic the most potent pheromones that humans release.

If you decide to make a custom blend, choose four, or fewer, essential oils and mix them in small amounts. This way, you can create several blends to complement the full range of emotions, wishes, and expectations that you have for your relationship. You must begin with a base oil — one tablespoon for every five drops of essential oil. If you have sunflower or olive oil in your cupboard, either will be fine, but you may prefer to use a more gently scented oil, like jojoba or coconut; almond oil has an interesting fragrance that may appeal to you. Add a few drops of the selected essential oils to the base. Start with two or three choices and, of course, use less of the stronger fragrances. Test the scent on your wrist and add a few drops more, if needed. Store the bottle in a dark cupboard, out of reach of children — these oils are for external use only. Let the blend mature for one week, and try to use it up within a month.

Here is one recipe for love you might have fun trying. Place one teaspoon of base oil in a small, clean jar. Add three drops of cinnamon oil, and shake well. Then add, in turn, three drops each of lavender oil, vanilla oil, and jasmine oil, shaking well after each addition. Store the blend in a dark cupboard for one week before using.

Once your special love blend has matured, you are ready to give or receive a massage. Massaging your partner can be nurturing, loving, erotic. The rubbing action will release the fragrance of the essential-oil blend, further heightening the mood of this affectionate exchange. Your favorite personal blend may be relaxing or stimulating—experiment to see which you both prefer. Use massage as a tool to increase intimacy, to learn about each other's bodies and touch preferences. Try several different techniques, for example:

Kneading: Place both hands on your partner, palms down. Press down with your palms while gently curling your fingers to gather flesh, just as you would when kneading bread dough.

Circling: Place both hands on your partner, palms down. Pressing down, make wide circular motions in a repeating pattern.

Effleurage: Position yourself behind your partner and place your hands lightly on his or her cheeks with your fingers pointing downward. Varying the pressure of your touch, slide your hands up towards your partner's ears and then back down again. You may use this stroking motion over your partner's entire body.

A complete massage will take about half an hour. It will take several hours for the oils to be absorbed into the body, so do not bathe during this time.

Make a special blend of essential oils to add to your bath water—baths that purify, relax, or stimulate are wonderful tools. Your oil blend will not dissolve in the water, but the steam that rises from the hot tub will carry the blend's potent fragrance and the heat will speed its absorption into your skin. (Remember to tie your hair back, as it will take several washes to remove any oil that gets into it.)

Alternatively, you can use the fragrant steam that rises from oil heated in hot water to give yourself a facial. To do this, bring a large pot of water to a boil, and pour the water into a bowl. Add three or four drops of your essential-oil blend. Hold your hand over the bowl for a moment to be sure that the steam is not too hot. When the steam reaches a soothing temperature, lean over the bowl and drape a towel over your head. Allow the aromatic steam to caress your face for a few minutes.

One final use for your favorite essential-oil blend is as a fragrance for lotions, shampoos, or creams. Choose an unscented product, preferably a lanolin-free one made from natural products, and mix in drops of oil until you have created a scent that suits you.

Pentacle and Pentagram

The pentagram is an ancient symbol of faith in the powers of the natural world. This five-pointed star depicts the four elements and the spirit. Imagine the forces of these five points merging together at the center of the pentagram and creating a mist of elemental powers wherein powerful magick can be wrought. The pentacle is the circular disc onto which the symbol of the pentagram is superimposed. It is the pentagram's sacred space. As a ceremonial tool—it is often used as a surface on which to set items that will be consecrated — the pentacle is feminine in nature and represents the earth element.

The pentagram and pentacle are among the many symbols with roots in the ancient world that you may choose to incorporate into your handfasting ceremony. There are symbols for an array of powers and elements, and they may be carved into candles, sewn into the hem of your handfasting attire, embroidered on the cloth, or embossed on the invitations.

Wand

A wand or scepter is a traditional tool in magickal ceremonies. Like the athame, it is used to direct energy. Wands can be made of wood or metal. If you should be so fortunate as to discover a tree that has been splintered by lightning, use a branch of it to make your wand — after all, it was carved by Nature herself! Engrave the wand with runes, or set crystals into it. Place a crystal at its most pointed end. When choosing crystals, carefully consider the types of energy that each represents and its elemental nature (see figure 14, page 92). Or, design a unique wand using quartz of various colors. This will create a powerful wand that vibrates at all color frequencies but within the harmonious structure of one crystal type.

Take the time to understand the magickal properties of the ceremonial tools and traditions available to be used in your handfasting. They will strengthen you as you enter the sacred space to enact your sacred union.

Man is a little piece of earth,
with a little piece of sky over him;
and all the laws of this outward earth and sky
are repeated in him on a larger scale.

—John Burroughs

Sacred Space & Divination

As dusk falls on Beltane Eve, a mossy doorway leading into the side of the hill slowly opens. Moments before, the door had been hidden, but now its wide opening reveals the mouth of a tunnel that spirals up from the depths of the earth. Pouring through the door is a host of creatures: lovely ladies in translucent gowns, flitting faeries as fragile as hummingbirds, and all manner of wee folk. They are coming from the otherworld to celebrate the union of the Goddess and the God. On this night, the gossamer-thin veil between the worlds has parted.

A handfasting is a sacred and magickal event. But if we are to experience its wondrous dimensions, we must possess an understanding of divinity and the tools to commune with the divine. Anyone can go through the motions of the ritual, but only those who embrace the divine, who accept it with their bodies, minds, and souls, will be able to enter the handfasting's sacred space and experience the magick. This chapter looks at ways of preparing a sacred space for your handfasting and at methods of drawing the divine into the ritual of your union.

SACRED SPACE

Whether they worshiped the moon or the sun, the ancients looked to the heavens for the points of reference they needed to define sacred space. The Roman word *templum* came to mean "temple," but it originally meant a space designated in the sky or on earth for the observation of omens and for divination. Often, a sacred space would be chosen by the gods themselves. They would indicate their wishes by marking a given spot with a natural sign: a bolt of lightning, an eruption of lava, the miraculous survival of an aged oak tree, a natural spring, or even a shoreline where earth and water danced to the tidal phases of the moon. Other times, the spiritual leaders of the community would consecrate a place and watch for signs that it had been accepted by the gods.

In all cultures, stones were used to mark sacred sites. At Delphi was situated the *omphalos*, or "navel" — a sacred stone symbolizing fertility and power. Zeus himself was believed to have deposited the stone there. He bade two eagles to fly to either end of the earth and then speed towards each other. The eagles reunited over Delphi, designating it as the center of the world. And Stonehenge, of course, is perhaps the most famous of the sacred stone monuments.

The ancient peoples of Western Europe were particularly enthusiastic about stone monuments. Although the earliest megalithic structures date back to about 3,000 B.C.E., earth-goddess figures found by archaeologists have been traced back to 20,000 B.C.E. Whatever their origins, megalithic monuments continue to generate the magick first instilled in them by their creators.

To the ancients, the world was a labyrinth of temporal and spatial possibilities. Omens were everywhere, and sacred spaces could be found in caverns where stalactites dripped from womblike walls; at the foot of volcanoes where the Earth Goddess gave birth to obsidian, volcanic glass, a razor-sharp gift to the devoted; beside bubbling natural springs that moistened the earth, nurturing new life; in groves of oak, hazel, or rowan, where the wisdom of the ancients resided in the concentric circles that told the age of each tree. Today, many people still believe in the wisdom of the ancients and share with their ancestors the recognition that nature is powerfully infused with divinity.

If you believe, as well, then consider consecrating a sacred site for your handfasting ritual. In choosing such a site, first consider the lore of ley lines and doorways. Irish legend holds that faery feet have worn paths between places of power and magick. These footpaths are called ley lines. Where two or more ley lines intersect, powerful energies meet. Ley lines, or lines of energy, form a kind of network throughout the world. Where they converge and intersect, sacred sites have been founded — Stonehenge and Glastonbury both stand on the line called St. Michael's Ley.

Doorways can be equally magickal. In mystical traditions, barriers must be erected to prevent unimpeded travel from one realm to another —

doorways, physical or symbolic, are needed. The Ancient Celts thought that at certain hours and at certain times of the year, Nature herself opened the door between this world and the next. The festivals of Beltane and Samhain were celebrations of her willingness to do this. At these times, when moon and sun, night and day, struck a balance, our world and the next approached a state of equilibrium. Magick, ritual, and divining could take place as Nature's portals opened. So, the doorways in ancient sacred spaces became powerful symbols of special access to another realm, a realm inhabited by the Goddess and the God.

Of course, it's unlikely that you will be able to celebrate your hand-fasting at a world-famous sacred site like Stonehenge; instead, you'll likely choose a place that has personal resonance for you and your part-ner and then consecrate it. When you cast a ritual circle, you create a sacred space. Within the protective boundaries of that space, you will be able to raise the energies of the natural and spiritual worlds to bless your union. The space is sacred because it is where the physical and the divine will meet and commune. It is a space of wonder and inspiration, awe and power.

If you are planning a small handfasting and inviting people who are comfortable with the ritual, then you may ask your guests to form the circle — or at least move inside the one you've created. If you are hosting a grand ceremony with a hundred guests, many of whom are not inti-mates, you will probably want to cast a small circle and seat the guests outside of it. Depending on your preferences, you may perform your casting in a highly ritualistic manner or in a casual, relaxed way.

To cast a circle of any size, you must purify yourself, draw the circle, purify the dedicated space, call upon the elements, and invite the God-dess and the God to attend. This is the preferred sequence, but you may want to alter it or to combine ritual tasks. This is fine — what matters most is that you create a space that is meaningful and magickal for you and your lover. You may decide to cast your circle prior to the handfast-ing ceremony, because you feel that some of your guests would be more comfortable with that arrangement.

However you choose to proceed, your first step will be to assemble your tools. Here is a suggested list: a measuring tape, some sage incense, a white feather, four candles (red, green, yellow, and blue), an athame or a wand, tokens to outline the circle (flowers, herbs, or branches).

Next, set up your altar and mark the circle around it. In determining the diameter of the circle, remember that multiples of three hold special power: nine feet — three by three — is particularly magickal. Make sure that the area is clean and uncluttered and that you will not be disturbed. Cleanse yourself, body, mind, and soul — perhaps with a ritual bath and meditation. You may also choose to mist those joining you in the casting with sea-salted water. Finally, purify the area with your besom, sage incense, and/or sea-salted water.

When these preparations are complete, step to the altar. Close your eyes, and meditate on the sacred space you wish to create and the divine presence you hope to invoke. Once you feel at peace and full of hope, you may begin the consecration ritual. Raise your athame or wand in your left hand to salute the heavens, the moon (the Goddess), and the sun (the God). Imagine the heavenly light filling you. Allow yourself to feel the celestial energies as they start to surround you. Imagine the golden or silvery glow (depending on whether you are casting under the sun or the moon) as an aura moving over and through your body. Sense its warmth. When you feel fully enveloped, lower your arm. Switch your athame/wand to your right hand. Extend your right arm and imagine the light force traveling through you, into the athame/wand, and then out into the circle. Walk clockwise around the circle as you direct the energy from the athame/wand that will delineate the sacred space's circumference. When you have completed the circle on the ground, lower your arm in an arc, sweeping it across the earth and raising it over your head; you have now created a protective three-dimensional sphere of earth and sky. Envision a shimmering veil of energy where you have cast your circle, a shield that will protect those you have invited and repel any negative forces. Recognize that you are between worlds, in a sacred place where communion with the Goddess and the God is possible. The potential of this place is as great as your faith in the magickal.

By forming this sphere, you have attracted the interest of the beings who inhabit the worlds of magick. Imagine these creatures as they turn their attention towards your activities. As your protective sage incense burns, walk three times around the circle, sending fragrant smoke wafting through the air by gently waving a white feather. Sketch magickal symbols in the air as you walk. You may also chant:

> This sacred space we purify
> For fire, water, earth, and sky
> With respect and reverence just
> In perfect love and perfect trust.

Now it is time to call the quarters, to invite the elementals, to raise your awareness and focus on their presence. You might also wish to call out an invitation to a beloved relative who has passed away. Begin your invocations to the south, in honor of the fires of Beltane. As you call the quarters, breathe deeply and sense the power and presence of the elementals.

While you are still in the south, stop. With your athame/wand, trace a pentagram in the air and call out:

> Hail guardians of the Southern Watchtower
> Fire and flames portend of your power
> You who set spirits afire
> And warm our hearts with passionate desire
> I invoke you, come to me!
> Be welcomed here. Blessed be.

Light the red candle. Feel the energy of their presence.

Move to the west and stop. With your athame/wand, trace a penta-gram in the air and call out:

Hail guardians of the Western Watchtower
Waves and whirlpools portend of your power
You who guide the flow of life sublime
Whose currents steer the ebb of time
I invoke you, come to me!
Be welcomed here. Blessed be.

Light the green candle. Feel the energy of their presence.

Move to the north and stop. With your athame/wand, trace a penta-gram in the air and call out:

Hail guardians of the Northern Watchtower
Quakes and volcanoes portend of your power
You who grant the world fertility
And reward with abundance and diversity
I invoke you, come to me!
Be welcomed here. Blessed be.

Light the yellow candle. Feel the energy of their presence.

Move to the east and stop. With your athame/wand, trace a penta-gram in the air and call out:

Hail guardians of the Eastern Watchtower
Tempests and tornadoes portend of your power
You who give flight to dreams and contemplation
You who breathe life into all of creation
I invoke you, come to me!
Be welcomed here. Blessed be.

Light the blue candle. Feel the energy of their presence.

The realm within the circle is not subject to linear time. It is a place where there are no beginnings and no ends. Envision the center of the circle as a cauldron of natural energy or a spiraling vortex. Feel the elements as they whirl around and through you in a magickal mist. Close your eyes and feel water's spray, gritty with earth's salt, carried on air's gentle breeze and warmed by fire's sunlight. At the handfasting, you will call on these four elemental powers to weave your two lives into one.

To call upon the Goddess and the God, use the swirling energy at the center of the circle, a place of magick and transformation. Choose the guises in which you want the deities to appear. It is best to compose your own invocation; keep it simple, and consider including phrases that can be repeated by the other members of your party. Here is one example to guide you:

Call out to her — Aphrodite*:

Glorious lady of beauty and desire
Great Goddess who kindles passion's hot fire
Moon Queen who rules fertility

Whose wisdom knows love's mystery
Join with us this handfasting to bless
For this couple bound by love and tenderness.

Call out to him — Adonis:

Magnificent lord of youth and desire
Great God whose potency is creation's fire
In your strength and virility
With your brilliant divinity
Come to us to witness this rite
Where lovers have chosen this day to unite.

*In handfastings, we often invoke the Goddess in the guise of one who is associated with love, sex, fertility, and procreation. Of course, you may choose a deity who represents other, equally meaningful values and natural forces, for example: Abundantia, prosperity and good fortune; Brigid, fertility and healing; Demeter, maternal devotion; Hecate, power and confidence (Goddess of Witchcraft); Hera, ambition; Hestia, domestic bliss; or Luonnotar, power of Nature.

Once the circle is cast, you may begin the ceremony (see chapter 6, The Ceremony: Your Vows and Ritual). If the circle has been cast prior to the service (due to a lengthy guest list or the presence of those who would be made ill at ease by the casting ritual), you and your partner must symbolically cut a doorway for your entry into the circle using the athame or wand. After stepping into the sacred space, remember to close the portal you've made with your ceremonial tool in order to contain the energies until it is time to commence the ritual. Ideally, however, the ceremony will begin as soon as the circle is cast.

What follows is a description of a circle casting that could be employed during a handfasting attended by a relatively small group of intimates. If you are planning such a handfasting, use this description as a basis on which to build your own special ceremony.

Altars are set at northern, southern, eastern, and western points in the perimeter of the circle; another is set in the circle's center. Guests have been asked to bring items that symbolize the four elements — feathers, poems, trinkets — and to place them on the appropriate altar. They then form a large circle and sit. The diameter of the circle is large enough to accommodate everyone comfortably. Next, the officiant explains the ceremony so that those who are unfamiliar with this kind of ritual will have a sense of what is happening. Four attendants, chosen prior to the ceremony, stand by their respective altars. Each, in turn (starting with the east, for new beginnings), invokes an element using invocations that they have written themselves; this allows the attendants — whether they be family members or close friends — a wonderful opportunity to be directly involved in the ritual. Once the four directions have been invoked, the officiant calls upon the spirits of the center. After the ceremony, the guests remain in the circle and the altar attendants, now in the opposite order, thank their respective elements and bid them farewell.

Whether you decide to cast your circle before or during the ceremony, you will need to make time for grounding. The term has two meanings when we are speaking of rituals and castings. First, it means to center yourself before the casting — to clear your mind of everyday worries through visualization or meditation so that you can focus on the ritual. Second, grounding means to bring yourself back to the everyday world after you have been transported by the ritual. Whenever we raise our awareness to commune with the Goddess and attune ourselves to the powerful forces of nature, we transform the energy in and around us. In the magickal space of the circle, our spirits soar, our burdens fall away, and we enter a realm of possibilities. It is not surprising that after such a whirlwind flight we feel light-headed. We need to sense the earth beneath our feet again, to ground our energy in everyday experience once more.

Food is a grounding tool, and feasting with others is a way to celebrate the journey our souls have taken, as well as the warm bond among those who have shared in the ceremony. In most traditions, a blessing is made over the food before it is eaten. A blessing like the Wicca Blessing of the Cakes and Wine may be offered at your handfasting as a simple appreciation of Nature herself; such a blessing is broad enough that it doesn't exclude guests of different religions. To perform it, hold up a little bread and a full goblet, and say:

> We give thanks for these gifts
> The beauty of Earth herself
> The fruits and grains of Nature
> The nectar of the gods
> We give thanks for this plenty
> And ask for your blessing
> On the feast before us.

With a ceremonial knife, cut a few crumbs from the bread and let them fall. Dip the knife into the goblet and let a few drops fall to the ground. If it seems practical, pass the bread and the goblet around so that everyone can sample a little of each; alternatively, use this rite to initiate a round of toasts and storytelling (some of your guests may have tales to tell about how you and your partner met!).

Another way to ground your spirit after the ceremony is, again, to use imagery and meditation. Stand with your eyes closed. As your spirit soars like a bird, envision yourself in feathered form. Land on a branch of a lush oak tree. Shift your thoughts to the tree itself. Feel the strength of the branch, inhale the fresh scent of the leaves. Feel your arms become branches. Imagine yourself as the living tree, the sap flowing through your veins. Feel the sap travel down your trunk. Sense your strength, your aged soul, your spirit eternal. Imagine your roots reaching deep into the rich earth; you are retaining the energy you need and releasing the excess into the earth, with thanks. Now, with your feet firmly planted, conscious of the life flowing through your body, remembering the sensation of flight, open your eyes. Feel well and refreshed.

When all participants in the ceremony have successfully grounded themselves, it is time to conclude the ritual by closing the circle. Rituals taking place inside the circle, the magickal sphere of natural energy, must be formally completed so that the energy within the space and within those beings in attendance — both human and divine — is released. First, thank the Goddess and the God with these words:

The magick is wrought, the rite is done
Oh, Lady of the Moon, Lord of the Sun
Great Goddess and God, farewell to thee
We give thanks for your presence. Blessed be.

Next, undo the casting of the circle by walking counterclockwise. At each quarter, snuff out the candle and remove any tokens you have placed there. As you extinguish each candle, thank the elemental in that quarter. Your thank-you can be as simple as this one:

Farewell guardians of the Southern Watchtower
Pray go in glory and in power
For your presence here, thanks to thee
We await your return. Blessed be.

If you still sense the energy in the sphere, hold the athame or wand in your left hand, at navel level, so that your chakra for absorbing personal power and experience is in line with the energy flow. Direct the athame towards the sphere. Close your eyes. Imagine the energy flowing from the circle boundary into the athame and back into you. Feel the circle force being drawn inside you. Know that the dominance of the protective sphere is giving way to the everyday world.

DIVINATION

A sacred space is one that has been prepared and consecrated for communion with the divine. This communion is practiced in ritual and in divination. Members of religions that do not have a sacred book seek instruction and direction through communion with the gods. Reading celestial movements, interpreting dreams, casting runestones or dice, and dowsing are all forms of divination that guide the faithful.

Divination is commonly thought of as the art of gaining insight into future events by inspiration, intuition, magick, or any supernatural means. But it is much more than merely reading the future: it is exploring the unknown. Divination is looking inward as much as it is looking forward; it is also looking back to karmic moments, and that experience can be the most mystical of all.

The Latin phrase *disciplina etrusca*, or "Etruscan science," refers to the whole body of work concerning the interpretation of the divine will through celestial signs, portents, and natural phenomena, as well as the rituals enacted for divine protection. Divination assumes that events occur in order to express a meaning. It also assumes that there are natural forces at work that guide and protect us. The challenge in divining is to understand and interpret the signs.

While divining can take many forms, you will probably find yourself drawn to one over another, so that is where you should begin your exploration. Just as each of us can find a way to express creativity — whether by painting a masterpiece or the walls of a bedroom — each of us can find a means to hone insight and intuition. What follows are descriptions of four divination methods that are relatively simple to use but have great potential for those who study them. The exercises that are offered here are meant to be fun and useful to you in your attempt to explore your love relationship and to enrich your handfasting experience.

Casting Dice

The first divination method is casting runestones, sticks, bones, or dice. This is an ancient practice. Many ancient cultures used a type of casting divination, often using objects with magickal runic characters and symbols engraved on them. The Ancient Celts, for example, carved the Ogham characters — precursors to runic forms — into their casting sticks in order to draw on the energies and qualities of trees for divination. The root of the word *rune* is associated with the concept of *secrets*, specifically the secrets and wisdom of magick and seership; in the Old English epic *Beowulf*, a *runwita* is a wise counselor to the king.

The word *runes* refers, in particular, to the markings used by the Celts and Anglo-Saxons, but it can mean any kind of magickal marking — for example, Egyptian hieroglyphics may be used in a form of casting divination that is both ancient and magickal.

Runestones are readily available to anyone interested in experimenting with them. Tarot cards and rune cards are also fascinating tools. If you would like to try a simple method of casting dice as part of your handfasting, consider these two:

Method: Draw a circle on a piece of white paper. Clasp three dice in your hands, concentrate on a question, and throw the dice onto the paper. Set aside the dice that land outside the circle; you will use those that land within it. Add the numbers appearing on the faces of the dice inside the circle. Check figure 16 (pages 132-33), Number Meaning, to determine the meaning of the number you come up with.

Method: Using figure 19 (page 144), Houses/Areas of Life, as your casting surface, clasp three dice in your hands; concentrate on a question, and throw the dice on the figure. Set aside the dice that land outside the circle; you will use those that land within it. First look at which house or area of life holds which numbers, then read the number meanings using figure 16 (pages 132-33). Do this for each die in each house, then add the numbers on the dice and read the general answer to your question.

In the case of both methods, odd numbers tend to indicate a no answer, and even numbers indicate a yes answer, but the meanings listed in figure 16, clarify the gray areas in between. Often, a no, or odd-number answer, is actually a warning that what you desire will only be realized if you give it your focused attention, whereas a yes, or even number answer, means that your wish will work itself out naturally, without any extra effort on your part. Imagine, for example, that using method 2 you ask, "Where shall we hold the celebration?" You then roll a four into the third house and a five into the fourth house. (The third die lands outside the circle.) The four in the third house indicates that you had better get to work on this issue and ask friends and relatives if they have any recommendations (third house), because time and effort will be required to get the location you want (number four). The five in the fourth house indicates that this is a very important issue for you (fourth house); you care a great deal about your handfasting location, and you will work to secure the right one, even though you will face some changes and challenges along the way (number five). Your efforts will pay off, and the results will be perfect (4 + 5 = 9). Your question isn't a yes-or-no one, and you have rolled an even number and an odd number, but the casting has predicted success — despite a few preliminary ups and downs.

Figure 16: Number Meaning

1. You will need to take the lead. Independence is of great concern. Expect a new beginning.
2. You will need to summon strength. Romance preoccupies you, but do not overlook the practical.
3. You will be blessed with good fortune. A magickal number, full of hope and potential. Expect good news and rewarded efforts.
4. You will work hard to overcome obstacles. Time and effort will be required to achieve security.
5. You will be passionate in this regard. Determination and drive will deliver success, but expect change along the way.
6. Pay attention to detail and routine tasks. Find pleasure in helping

others, and peace of mind will be your reward.

7. Expect a magickal experience. Attend to your spiritual needs.

8. Circumstances will be extreme, but the changes will bring needed balance to your life. Whether a success or a failure, it will be pronounced. Avoid borrowing money, if possible, during this transition period.

9. Expect material and spiritual success. A charmed number.

Separate and add numbers above nine; for example, eighteen is one plus eight, equaling nine. In some traditions, eleven is viewed as a particularly lucky number, bringing success in all endeavors.

Dream Interpretation

The second divination method is dream interpretation. The Ancient Chaldeans were among the first to record dream interpretations, but all ancient peoples, including the Druids, practiced this art. In Druidic tradition, a question would be put to an initiate. The initiate would then enter a space sacred to the Goddess and lie down on a bullhide — an object sacred to the God — where he or she would sleep or meditate until a dream sequence unfolded. An interpreter would then read the signs contained in the dream and reveal its hidden answer to the initiate. In some cultures, dream experience was thought to be as real as waking experience. If one dreamed one was a bird, soaring above the plains, that meant that one had truly shapeshifted to become the spirit of the bird.

Dreams take us on a journey into our own spirits. They are filled with symbols that seem to offer intensely personal messages. Even if you have a dream that appears relevant to others — such as a precognitive dream — the emotional impact of key images in the dream is unique to your personal experience. A dream is a message sent to you, and only you can fully understand it. Its internal logic holds meaning for you, exclusively.

All significant dream symbols have an emotional dimension that will guide the dreamer to a message. Many symbols are very clear: for example, dawn represents a new beginning, storm clouds represent stress, ladders represent an opportunity to rise above a given situation. Your unconscious mind chooses symbols or images that have special meaning for you, and it uses these to communicate with your conscious self.

As you plan your handfasting, you are likely to have many dreams. Your world is in transition, you are poised on the threshold of a whole new life, ready to commit yourself to another. It is a wonderful time to take guidance from within. Whether that guidance is coming to you through meditation or night dreams, learn to interpret its rich meaning. The first thing you must learn to do is invoke dream messages. You may choose to work with scrying techniques or to simply direct yourself to have, and remember, night dreams. In either case, you will have to relax your mind and body, breathe deeply, and focus on the process of dreaming or the topic that you would like to dream about.

If you elect to try scrying, or trance, techniques, then you will be engaging in a practice used by Nostradamus. The renowned astrologer would gaze into a steaming brass cauldron laced with herbs and dream his visions of the future. This is called scrying, and the medium can be water, fire, or crystal; the scrier must simply stare, in a relaxed state, at a reflective surface until he or she becomes entranced and susceptible to visions. To scry, follow these steps: choose a scrying medium, say water. Illuminate your space with candles. Scent the space with burning sage and chamomile. Relax. Breathe deeply. Look both at, and past, the water. Focus on your meditation, but do not close your eyes. At first, images may appear only in your mind's eye, but, with practice, you will be able to make them appear on the scrying surface. Do not force the images or push yourself to understand them during the trance. Just experience the vision — interpretation comes later.

If you decide to invite night dreams for interpretation, you will be attempting a process of self-hypnosis. To do this, prepare for bed and get into a comfortable sleeping position. Close your eyes. Tell yourself that you will count to three slowly, and that as you do you will imagine yourself walking down three stairs. Tell yourself that on each stair you will deposit a box of worries but that you can pick them up again in the morning, if need be. Breathe very deeply. Feel your chest expand as you inhale. As you exhale, let your chest relax and feel the tension exit your body with your breath. Imagine your feet as you descend the three stairs. See yourself setting down the boxes of worries. There is no need to look inside the boxes; just feel the tension in your body diminishing as you deposit each one. (Later in the process, if a concern pops into your head — like tomorrow's big meeting — stuff it into a box and drop-kick it onto a stair.) Tell yourself that as you go down the stairs you are becoming more relaxed and are drifting deeper and deeper into a state of self-hypnosis. At the bottom of the stairs, turn and look back to assure yourself that you have left your cares behind. Tell yourself that you will dream tonight, and that you will remember the dreams when you awake. Turn forward again, and see a door in front of you engraved with the words "Sleep and Remember."

Open the door. See a steaming bathtub filled with luscious golden liquid. Imagine yourself slipping into the warm bath. Feel your feet in the liquid, warmed and relaxed. Concentrate on the feeling in your feet. Let them become so relaxed that you cease even to feel them. See a warm gold mist rise from your feet like an aura and envelop your entire body.

Know that you are safe and protected. Settle into the bath, imagining each part of your body relaxing and drifting away from your awareness. When you have fully immersed yourself in the liquid, understand that your body is so relaxed that it is of no concern. If you are already asleep, choose an endless, gently moving image — soaring through the air, riding an escalator to the heavens, gliding through waves — and let it carry you to the world of dreams. Any method of relaxation takes practice. Be patient, and you will eventually succeed.

Record your dreams as soon as you wake. Note the images, feelings, dialogue — as much detail as possible. Remember that your dream images are symbols, and they rarely mean what they initially suggest. Do not be dismayed by images that at first seem negative — they are usually a form of guidance, and they can assist you in areas of your life that need attention. As you prepare to interpret the dream images you have recorded in the weeks leading up to your handfasting, pay special attention to those that have particular significance for lovers: birds, chasing, hands, houses, roads, the moon and sun. Let's look at what these can mean and consider what questions they can raise.

Birds are said to be harbingers of good news coming down from the heavens. But note the color and type of the bird you dream about. Do birds have any personal associations for you? Does a particular type of bird bring a certain person to your mind? Watch the action of the bird. A bird that eats from your hand is quite different from one that swoops to peck at your head. A white dove that brings you a twig is offering a gift of future harmony and peace. A scarlet cardinal that arrives with its mate to build a nest might foretell the love and commitment that your handfasting will nurture. In all dreams, look for the subtleties as well as the broad themes.

If you dream of chasing, are you chasing or being chased? What are you chasing? What is chasing you? Is it a game, or are you fearful? Do you want to turn to face your pursuer? Is this image a warning? Are you delaying or trying to escape something in your everyday life?

Handfasting lovers are especially likely to dream about hands. Notice what the hands you dream of are doing in order to understand the message this image carries about your union. Are the hands working? Caressing? Signing a lease? Changing a diaper?

A lover who dreams about a house is receiving a message about personal finances and domesticity. The house is a symbol of safety and permanence. Is the house you envision cozy and well furnished, a site for domestic bliss and financial security? Or is it a dilapidated trailer, a place where worries about commitment and money reside? What do you notice most about the house? Where is it located? Is there anyone else inside it? Is the house familiar?

Dream images of the moon and sun are generally positive ones. These celestial bodies are sources of illumination; they light our way. Moonlight, despite its association with darkness, does not signify evil — it is creative, magickal, and mysterious. Sunlight is warm and comforting; its golden radiance is a sign of prosperity and good fortune. These images are good omens, since they are representations of the gods.

A road is a wonderful image for a handfasting couple. Is the road you dream of smooth? Does it hold any obstacles? If so, what is the nature of those obstacles? Can you see to the end of the road? Does the route wind or curve? What do you see on the sides of the road? Who is traveling with you?

Whatever symbols you are presented with as you dream, take the time to think through their personal associations. How do these symbols make you feel? What other thoughts do they lead you to? How do they fit into the big picture of your dream?

Pendulum Divination

The third divination method is pendulum divination, or dowsing. This practice affords us the opportunity to come into close contact with the intuitive side of our natures, the side that is capable of sensing the forces that are at work around us. Because of this, pendulum divination can be an exciting way to investigate love relationships and, more specifically, to make handfasting choices.

As it is with any divination technique, the important thing about pendulum divination is not only the results it brings. Another crucial aspect is the question that you pose. If you direct the pendulum to answer the question, "Does she love me," the question itself may reveal your unconscious insecurities. Consider first what you want to ask, how you will word the question, how strongly you feel about the question and its answer; only then should you examine the pendulum's revelations.

Pendulum divination is like rod divining and other such techniques in that it allows the practitioner access to the unconscious mind, the realm where memory, intuition, and psychic ability operate unhindered by the type of restrictions imposed by our conscious minds. As the pendulum swings, messages and answers — whether they be emotional responses or psychic impressions — are sent from the unconscious through the autonomic nervous system to the muscle reflexes. You, yourself, are moving the pendulum, but do not let this disappoint you. The forces of the spirit, the energies of the natural world, are working through you. Surely, it is far more exciting to sense the divine within you, acting in harmony with the essence of your individuality, than it is to imagine some ghostly form controlling the divining object swaying beneath your hand.

To practice this technique, you may use a readily available item — a pendant necklace or a needle on a thread. To empower the pendulum with a more concentrated quantity of your personal energy, use your handfasting ring or a necklace given to you by your lover. If you want to create a special pendulum, purchase a small chunk of crystal and a twelve-inch chain or some thread to suspend it from. Amethyst is an ideal crystal choice for pendulum divination. Its purple hue is a color vibration of the third eye, and its magickal properties enhance our ability to drift between states of consciousness.

For yes-or-no questions, any pendulum you choose will be fine. For more advanced divination, you will need a pendulum with a fine point, because your magickal space will be filled with information. Once you have your pendulum, take it in your right hand and hold it to your heart. Imagine a white light, your aura, moving from you into the pendulum, and concentrate on filling it with your personal energy.

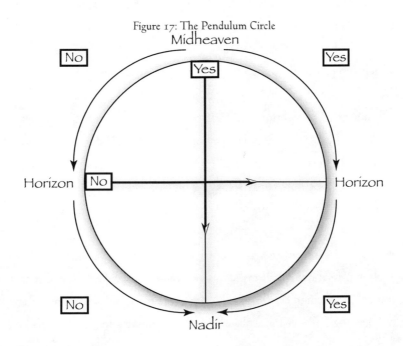

Figure 17: The Pendulum Circle

You are now ready to create the pendulum space. For simple yes-or-no questions, use figure 17 (page 139), The Pendulum Circle. For a more complex divination — to be undertaken by those who have practiced this art and are capable of attuning themselves to the natural energies they summon — a more elaborate space must be readied. This space will be a half circle, rather than a full circle. On a piece of paper, draw a half circle and mark pie-slice divisions on it. Label each slice with a category; you must repeat the category on the axis crossing the circle (because the pendulum will swing from side to side, across the full axis). As you create your pendulum space, think about your question. There are endless possibilities: for example, turn to figure 2 (page 34), Celtic Lunar/Tree Astrology Wheel, and select woods to be used in the construction of your besom; enter each on a pie slice.

Once you have prepared the pendulum and the pendulum space, you must formulate the question. This is not as simple as you might think. It must be a question that you have considered thoroughly, a question to which you genuinely want a truthful answer. And it must be very clear.

To begin with, pose a yes-or-no question. Be aware that the answer will not be as straightforward as it seems; you will have to interpret it carefully. If you ask, "Will we live happily ever after?" does a no answer mean that you will be perpetually unhappy? Does a yes answer mean that you will be constantly happy? This is a poorly worded question, and so its answer has no meaning because it has too many possible meanings.

There are several ways to construct a good question. One is to anchor it in time: "Will my dress be ready this Friday?" Or, direct it towards a specific person: "Will Liam agree to be my attendant for the handfasting?" Or, name a place: "Will our handfasting be held at The

Old Mill?" Make sure that the question is not subject to the will of others, and ensure that it is quite specific. Practical questions about your
handfasting — where, when, financial considerations, guests, and attendants — will work well. If you are determined to pose a question about
love, avoid one like, "Does she love me?" Instead, formulate a specific
one: "Will she tell me she loves me today?"; or, "Will she go out with
me this Saturday?"

There are several reasons why general questions do not give satisfac-
tory answers. One of the more interesting explanations is that the wording of your question is such that the answer can be interpreted in
several ways. This is called a Delphic response. When Croesus, King of
Lydia, consulted the oracle regarding his chances of defeating Cyrus
the Great of Persia, the oracle replied, "If you attack, a great empire will
fall." Croesus confidently went off to battle, little realizing that his own
empire was the one that would be destroyed. Another interesting ex-
planation for the inadequacy of general questions is that life is an inter-
play of fate and free will. Often, general questions do not yet have their
answers written in the stars. The way a situation develops can depend
entirely on choices made by those involved in it. Sometimes, even the
clearest question will yield an unreadable answer — the pendulum will
not begin to swing in one direction, or it won't swing at all. This means
that there is as yet no clear answer. Ask the question again later.

When you are ready to practice pendulum divination, gather your
tools. Lay your pendulum circle out on a flat surface, and get your pendulum, your list of questions, and a pen and paper with which to note
your results. Take a moment to relax, or perhaps to meditate. As you
will be asking questions relating to your love or your handfasting, you
must hold the pendulum to your heart, breathing deeply and clearing
your mind.

Next, hold the pendulum between your thumb and your index finger. Place your elbow firmly on the table. Suspend the pendulum over the circle's midpoint, without touching the surface. Concentrate on your initial yes-or-no question. Wait. If the pendulum begins to swing clockwise, or up and down (like a head shake yes), the answer is yes. If the pendulum begins to swing counterclockwise, or back and forth across the horizon (like a head shake no), the answer is no. If the pendulum does not move at all, or if its movements are unclear, then re-think the question, or wait until a later date and ask it again.

Astrology

The fourth divination method is astrology. The soul of astronomy, astrology is an ancient occult art, the study of cosmic forces as they manifest themselves in celestial bodies and their interactions. Lovers, in particular, find it very beneficial to gain an understanding of the cycles of the moon and the influences of the planets. Astrological charts can offer fascinating insights into the nature of relationships, their strengths and weaknesses.

While drawing up an astrological chart may be more time-consuming than, for example, casting dice, the rewards are great. Wait for a rainy afternoon, assemble some colored pencils, some paper, and a ruler, then go ahead and indulge your curiosity. However, before you actually start to construct the chart, you should familiarize yourself with its various elements. First, all astrological charts are circular — that is, 360 degrees. Those 360 degrees are divided to accommodate twelve zodiac signs (Aries through Pisces) — see figure 18 (page 143), The Zodiac. Each sign takes 30 degrees.

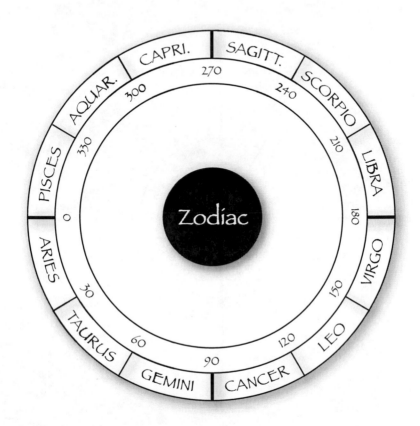

Second, all astrological charts include twelve houses representing different aspects of life, such as family, finances, career, and so on — see figure 19 (page 144), Houses/Areas of Life.

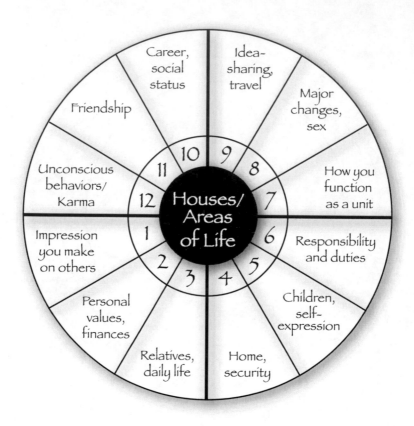

It is helpful to understand the symbolism of an astrological chart. Imagine yourself, at the moment of your birth, at the center of the circle. You look up into the heavens. A number of factors — for instance, the time of your birth — have determined which zodiac sign you see directly overhead and which zodiac sign you see on the horizon. The houses surrounding you are stationary, while the zodiac wheel rotates through the heavens and around the circle that you occupy. The planets and the luminaries (the moon and the sun) appear in the houses and zodiac signs that are inscribed over and around you.

To construct your own composite astrological chart, begin by acquiring the natal charts of you and your partner, which you can download for free from various Internet sites. You will have two charts in front of you that resemble figure 18 (page 143), with the planets and luminaries added. Trace figure 18 onto a piece of paper and cut it out; you will need to spin the wheel of the zodiac to align a sign with the correct house.

Remembering that a composite chart is a chart of midpoints, consult your natal charts and use the information they provide to locate your sun and your partner's sun on figure 18. Find the midpoint: that midpoint is your shared, composite sun. Then look at your moon and your partner's moon and find the midpoint between these bodies: that midpoint is your composite moon. Simply count the degrees between the two to find the middle position. Continue through all of the planets. If this procedure seems unclear, try approaching it this way. Say that your sun is at 4 degrees into Gemini and your partner's is at 6 degrees into Leo. Place a finger on figure 18 at 4 degrees of Gemini (or 64 degrees into the circle). Place a second figure at 6 degrees of Leo (or 126 degrees into the circle). Can you see that the midpoint between your sun and your partner's sun is 5 degrees of Cancer? That is, the composite-chart sun is at 5 degrees of Cancer.

When you have completed your list of composite planet positions, set it aside. Look at your Internet natal charts. Each will have a line that represents the beginning, or cusp, of the tenth house. Each chart may have a small number 10 in that house, or the word "Midheaven" may appear on the line itself. This line will occur at a specific degree on the circle. Find the midpoint between the cusp of your tenth house and the cusp of your partner's tenth house. This will be the line on your composite chart that runs from the top center of the chart to the bottom center.

Your composite tenth-house cusp will be in a sign and at a degree. Say, for example, it is 15 degrees of Cancer, which would be 105 degrees on figure 18. Now, position the zodiac wheel — the figure 18 that you have traced out of this book — so that 105 is at the top center. Tape the wheel into place. Make every house 30 degrees. In the example used here, that means that the tenth house will begin at 15 degrees of Cancer, the eleventh at 15 degrees of Leo, the twelfth at 15 degrees of Virgo, and so on. Shade these degrees with your colored pencils.

Next, draw a line from the tenth-house cusp degree — 105 or 15 degrees of Cancer — straight across to 15 degrees of Capricorn (285). The eleventh-house cusp would go from 15 degrees of Leo (135) to 15 degrees of Aquarius (315). Continue until you have split the circle into twelve pie slices; label these twelve house divisions according to figure 19 (page 144).

Finally, take your list of composite planet positions again, and mark the planets on the composite chart. For example, place a sun at 16 Capricorn at degree 286 in the chart. Well done! Now you are ready to interpret.

Equipped with your customized composite chart, consult the following two lists — Planets and Luminaries, and Zodiac Signs — to gain a valuable understanding of your sacred union. Each list indicates the special insights offered by the various planets and signs in relation to their positions on your composite chart. Notice how your expression as a couple differs from your expression as an individual. Look for balance in the four elements. To maximize this experience, write out a description for each of the planets, then consider what you, as a couple, must do to enhance your compatability.

PLANETS AND LUMINARIES

Consider how the planets listed below interact with the houses of signs.

Sun: the nature of the energy in your relationship, and how it appears to others.

Moon: the emotions at work in your relationship, and how you express these emotions as a couple.

Venus: the nature of your love and attraction, and your ability to express yourselves through love and affection.

Mercury: the quality of your communication, your ability to effect each other's thinking, and the extent to which you share ideas and viewpoints.

Mars: how your individuality continues to be expressed in the relationship, and how your two egos interact.

Jupiter: the areas in which you, as a couple, will learn and grow, and the nature of the experiences that will teach you and enrich your relationship.

Saturn: how you will need to plan and impose order together. The challenge to interpreting Saturn's position is to find ways to structure and define your relationship and determine the rules that you wish to impose on the relationship without making either of you feel that your freedom is being curtailed.

Uranus: the areas in which each of you most needs to feel unrestrained and creative.

Neptune: the intuitive understanding of each other's consciousness and dreams; how, as a couple, you can use idealism to attain exciting and meaningful goals.

Pluto: where your greatest challenges as a couple lie; the nature of those challenges, and the strengths you will both use to overcome them.

ZODIAC SIGNS

 ARIES: where this sign falls in the chart, you, as a couple, will find it easy to be enthusiastic and spontaneous. You will thrive on newness and anticipation. Aries's fiery energy pushes lovers to act on impulse. Aries offers excitement and romance, but look to other signs to find the strength to settle down, commit, and plan.

TAURUS: where this sign occurs, you will find the ability to build strong foundations. The slow growth of Taurean love leaves couples time to enjoy the sensual pleasures of the world and of their love as it blossoms. Taurus is where you can plan and commit, but guard against being inflexible in this area.

GEMINI: you can communicate and share ideas where Gemini occurs. Fun and variety will dominate this area of your life together. You will generate wonderful ideas, but be sure that they have substance.

CANCER: you will need to create a nurturing environment where Cancer falls in your chart. The comforting and affectionate nature of Cancer is needed, because in this area of your life you will feel insecure as a couple. Although Cancer's outward expression is reassuring and nurturing, Cancerian currents fluctuate beneath the surface. Expect to feel insecure in your Cancer house; it is an area of life where together you need to build confidence. By using Cancerian strengths to create a strong emotional bond, by supporting each other, you will find the strength to face the challenges the house presents.

LEO: where this signs falls in the chart, you shine as a couple. The way you both deal with this area of your life will likely be what others notice about you. Here, you are generous, charming, and probably lucky. Be careful not to let the positive rewards you reap from this area of your life distract you from addressing your shared needs in the other houses of the chart.

VIRGO: here, you will need to be charitable. Challenges and worries in this house will broaden your experience and your capacity for empathy. What we give, we will get back threefold; do not ignore this house.

LIBRA: confusion reigns where this sign falls in your chart. Do not be fooled by the astrological glyph of the balanced scales. Try to use those scales, and you will see that they dip this way and that — rarely do they achieve a balance. This is an area of life where you, as a couple, will have to avoid overindulgence as you search for equilibrium. Here, you will care deeply about being fair and finding the right focus for your energies; you will also need to practice tolerance, patience, and moderation to achieve harmony.

SCORPIO: where Scorpio falls in your chart, you will discover passion. It could be passion for each other, for your children, for your work, for your morning coffee; Scorpio is intense about absolutely everything. In your Scorpio house, you can both expect to be very serious. You will feel a great desire to control all matters, but concentrate your energies on attaining positive goals. Scorpio rules death and rebirth, a positive cycle of rejuvenation, and it is essential that as a couple you focus on the whole cycle. Think of tearing down old ideas or inhibitions as a step towards building something better, not as an act of destruction. Be introspective, analyze your habits, and accomplish personal growth through change in the house that Scorpio rules — this is the dynamic, positive expression of this sign.

SAGITTARIUS: you will both be optimistic and fortunate where this sign falls in your chart. In this house, you and your partner possess common sense, perhaps even wisdom. You can see how to make positive strides in this area of your life. But ensure that your dreams have substance, that you're not merely relying on your positive attitudes to carry your plans forward.

CAPRICORN: you will face challenges where this sign occurs, but, in overcoming them you may reap great rewards. In the Capricorn house, you must organize yourselves and plan. You have a great opportunity for prosperity here, but you must advance one step at a time. Be patient and persistent.

AQUARIUS: unexpected flashes of insight, unusual events, and unpredictable moments characterize this sign's placement. Aquarius invites us to expand our consciousness — here, we are meant to break out of old forms and routines to embrace creative choices. As a couple, where you find Aquarius you are likely to feel rebellious against the way others do things. The challenge is to act on those feelings in a way that benefits everyone; teach, rather than attack, and others won't label you as eccentrics.

PISCES: where Pisces falls in your chart, you will encounter the religious or spiritual depths of your union. What do you believe and understand as a couple in relation to the mystical? What areas of your life will this impact? The challenge is to find the flexibility to expand, learn, and grow together through an emotional and spiritual sharing of your beliefs, without imposing your truths on each other.

How but in custom and in ceremony
Are innocence and beauty born?
—William Butler Yeats, "A Prayer for My Daughter"

The Ceremony:
Your Vows & Ritual

As the guests move towards the sacred handfasting space, the subtle scent of rose, mingled with a hint of sage, welcomes them. Strains of harp music guide them to the doorway. They pass through, under a protective garland, and the more observant among them catch a glimpse of a pewter horseshoe tucked among the petals. Within, towards the north end of the room, draped in white satin and laid with various objects of silver and rose, they see the altar. The room is dimly lit and accented with candles. The guests make their way to their seats.

The ceremonial circle is before them, surrounding the altar. The circle is defined by small hills of white garden stones, sparkling in the candlelight, alternated with bouquets of wildflowers and herbs. A generous opening at the front of the circle will allow the couple to pass through without disturbing the objects that mark the circle's perimeter.

Two white candles in crystal holders sit at opposite ends of the altar surface. One large dusty-rose candle sits between these. A crystal bowl holds rose petals and sea salt. A very small dish contains an ounce of rose oil. Another little dish holds an ounce of sage oil. A white candle burns in a pewter cauldron. A wee bell and a crystal goblet of red wine also rest upon the altar. White cords have been draped across the altar's surface. The rings are there, too—but the guests can't see them, because they have been folded into a white satin cloth.

The harpist pauses. The handfasting couple is about to enter.

This chapter is devoted to the object of all your careful planning and preparation: the handfasting ritual itself. First comes a look at some sample handfasting vows and advice on how to write your own. The second part of this chapter is a sample ceremony to guide you as you create your own sacred and magickal ritual. Finally, several variations on that sample ceremony are offered.

THE VOWS

Marriage is the union of two divinities that a third might
　be born on earth.
It is the union of two souls in a strong love for the abolishment
　of separateness.
It is that higher unity which fuses the separate unities
　within the two spirits.
It is the golden ring within a chain whose beginning is a
　glance, and whose ending is Eternity.
It is the pure rain that falls from an unblemished sky, to
　fructify and bless the fields of divine Nature.

　　　　　　　　—Kahlil Gibran, *The Prophet*

Choosing appropriate and heartfelt vows will go a long way towards making your handfasting an intimate and unique experience. Whether you find a poem or other piece of writing that touches you or you decide to express your deepest emotions in your own way, the words you use must have meaning to both you and your partner. These words, as many ancient cultures believed, will have the power to bind your two lives together; they will interlock to form a promise, an oath, a vow.

You have many options for your ceremony: a favorite poem that speaks to your heart; a simple declaration, such as, "I love you with all my heart"; some special song lyrics. Or, if you sense that you will be too nervous to speak, choose another way to express what you feel: ask a friend to read a piece; play a recorded song; make a gesture of tenderness and respect, such as holding your partner's palm against your heart.

As you prepare to choose your vows or set them down on paper, think about the meaning that you and your lover want to bring to your ritual, as well as the powerful magick of the words that will express it. But take some time, as well, to ponder the following practical considerations.

First, are you planning to commit to one another for one year and a day, for a lifetime, for eternity, or for as long as the love shall last? The answer to this will affect the way you write your vows and what you want the officiant to say. There are many lovely ways to address this question of time that in no way undermine the importance of the handfasting. You may say, for example:

We make this commitment
For as long as the love shall last
For a year and a day

For a lifetime
For always
For all of time
Through eternity
Forever

Or, as long as you and your partner fully understand the nature of your oath, you can leave out references to a specific time period altogether, focusing instead on the act of uniting:

We join to each other
We are bound together
We will travel destiny's path together
Our love binds us
Today, we are united as one

Second, go over the wording of your vows together to ensure that its implications are precise. For example, are you "giving yourself" to your lover, or are you "taking a partner"? This is important, because if you say, "I will give myself to you," and your lover says, "I will take you," then your lover is left out of the equation; you give yourself, and you are received, but what does your lover give?

Third, review the section of chapter 1 titled The Legality of Handfasting. It may be that you have to incorporate specific phrases in your vows in order to make them legally binding.

The fourth practical consideration that you should address in writing your ceremony is whether you have any special acknowledgments to make. Your handfasting ritual may be the perfect occasion to commemorate a dear friend or family member who has recently passed away. Or perhaps there are elements of your religion that you would like to include. Also, ask yourselves whether it would seem appropriate to explain concepts that have significance to you as a couple — such as fate — to your guests in the context of the ceremony.

Fifth, decide whether the two of you will recite the vows. The alternative would be to have an officiant do most of the talking. Reflect on what would make you both feel most comfortable and relaxed. Also, think about whether you want your guests to participate in any way: a friend could give a reading; or everyone present could answer questions put to them by the officiant — for example, "Will you support this couple in their union?"

The sixth consideration is the tone of the language you use. Do you want the wording of the ceremony to be elaborate and romantic or simple and eloquent? Do you prefer strong, poetic language or a more moderate mode of expression? Remember to consider the tone of the ceremony from your guests' perspective, as well.

Seventh, decide how long you want the ceremony to last. It must be long enough to honor the importance of your handfasting, but not so long that it tries the patience of your guests. Fifteen to thirty minutes, depending on the complexity of the ritual, is a comfortable duration for most. Allow another thirty minutes for the arrival, seating, and departure of your guests, and your handfasting ceremony will last about an hour. Then it's time for the celebration!

Once you've thought through all of these considerations, you will probably have formed a relatively clear mental picture of the oath-taking part of your ritual. Do you envision reciting vows that you have penned yourselves? If so, keep it simple, be honest, and allow your true feelings to surface. What follows is a series of seven examples that may inspire you. (The last two are designed to be spoken by an officiant; the first five are to be spoken by the handfasting couple.) Perhaps you'll find among them a phrase or two that would suit your ceremony:

1. I cherish you
   And I cherish this precious love that we share
   This is my oath, my promise to be at your side
   Through the joys and the challenges
   That our life together brings
   Today, I choose to bind my life to yours, so that tomorrow
   And for many tomorrows, we will continue this life
   Together, as one
   I love you.

❀ ❀ ❀

2. Today, I choose to entwine my heart and spirit with yours
   To join as one, united in love
   This rebirth in love is natural
   As natural as the new life that burgeons forth each spring
   Just as the great oak tree, strong and alive, grows to unite the
      earth and the sky
   So steadfast love and devotion will hold us one to another.

❀ ❀ ❀

3. Destiny has made our paths to cross
   Today, hand in hand, I choose to walk through this life with you
   Or love was born to be, hearts as one
   All witness my oath to stay at your side forever.

❀ ❀ ❀

4. Today, I bind myself to you

   I promise to cherish and protect you through each day of my life

   Our love will bring passion and we will be warmed by desire

   Our friendship will banish loneliness and bring lifelong
      companionship

   Our fidelity and commitment will bind us ever unto each other

   With this handfasting, I choose to be joined as one with you

   From this day forward, we will be

   Trusting friends

   Faithful partners

   And each other's true soulmate.

❀ ❀ ❀

5. In our life together, I pledge to respect and honor you

   I swear that my love is true

   I will support you always as friend, lover, and confidante

   I will share your hopes and help to make your dreams come true

   I will stand by you in the good times and the bad

   I will cherish and protect you always.

❀ ❀ ❀

6. These two people have chosen a lifetime of love. Today, Brigid and
   Bran pledge their love and proclaim their union. As witnesses, we
   honor their oath and will support them in their lives together. Now,
   let Brigid and Bran join their souls in a partnership to last a lifetime.

❖ ❖ ❖

7. Nature finds no greater pleasure than in a couple's loving union. The joining of hearts, bodies, minds, and souls is a celebration of the path Nature has set us upon. With this handfasting, Brigid and Bran are bound together for life's seasons of love. In the spring of their love, they will explore each other. Their senses will bud with the newness and potential of their heart match. By the midsummer of their love, full-blossomed devotion will offer a rich harvest — children, prosperity, challenges, and rewards. The autumn of love promises the harvest of dearest friendship and mature passion. And, finally, when the pure white snows of winter blanket the earth of their lives, Brigid and Bran will rejoice at the lifetime of love they have shared and be warmed by the deep bond made here today, which still holds them. Today, we rejoice with Brigid and Bran as they proclaim their everlasting love.

As you compose your vows, here is a vocabulary for you to draw on:

- Words to express attractiveness: beautiful, fair, lovely, graceful, charming, elegant, noble, dignified, glorious, wondrous, worthy, handsome, lovable, loving, enchanting.
- Words to express affection and emotion: love, passion, yearning, longing, desire, kindle, refresh, adore, honor, cherish, treasure, prize, rarity, admire, respect, patience, forgiveness, appreciate, esteem, value, delight, nurture, devote, dedicate, bliss, joy, peace, harmony, happiness, pleasure, contentment, hope, inspiration, precious, divine, sublime, tender, gentle, serene.

- Words to express promise and honesty: pledge, vow, swear, plight (one's troth), join, unite, bind, handfast, wed, wedlock, marry, trust, fidelity, knowledge, oath, purity, sincere, earnest, loyal, faithful, genuine, steadfast, true, heartfelt, unwavering.
- Words to express duration: eternal, always, forever, undying, life-long, endless, timeless, infinite, destiny, fate, everlasting, ever after, infinity.
- Words to express partnership: couple, union, partner, mate, soulmate.

THE RITUAL

You've committed your vows to paper, and now you are ready to fit them into the framework of the ceremony. You may use the description of the handfasting ceremony given here as a blueprint for your own ritual, or merely as a general source of inspiration. Either way, your handfasting ritual should reflect your dreams and individuality. Improvise, be creative, enjoy the experience, and make it your own. (Although the terms *bride* and *groom*, *maid* and *groomsman* have been used in the following section for the sake of clarity, no sexist connotations are intended and no bias against same-sex couples is implied.)

A Sample Ceremony

When all the guests have arrived, the officiant moves to the back of the altar, and the harpist pauses. The officiant asks the guests to stand. The handfasting party enters, the groomsman leading the procession. Next comes the couple, walking side by side, groom on the right, bride on the left. The maid follows, carrying the broom, or besom. The groomsman enters the circle and stands to the right of the altar. The couple enters and stands directly before the altar. The maid stands to the left of the bride.

The officiant says, "Welcome all to the handfasting of Brigid and Bran. We gather here in perfect love and perfect trust to witness this sacred union. You may sit." The officiant pauses, then continues, "We come to this consecrated place with our hearts full of hope and good wishes for this couple's happy union. The maid will now close the circle with the ceremonial broom." The maid sweeps once and then places the broom across the circle's opening.

Dipping a stir stick into a vessel of sage oil, the officiant lets a few drops fall on the flame of a candle burning inside a pewter cauldron, saying, "This circle is purified with sage and has been swept clean so that only positive natural energies remain. Brigid and Bran will now light their own candles."

The lovers step up to the altar and light one candle each. As they do this, the officiant declares, "Let these candles symbolize the unique individuality of each of these people. They have come to this sacred site as two. They will now light the unity candle to symbolize their wish to join as one."

With their own candles, the bride and groom light the unity candle as the officiant says, "The element of fire is represented by these candles. May the bond between Brigid and Bran be forged in passion: a passion for each other, a passion for the life they share, and a passion for the commitment they make to each other here today." The bride and groom step back to their places.

The officiant takes a few drops of rose incense and lets them fall on the flame of the cauldron candle, saying, "The element of air is represented by this rose-scented smoke. May you share dreams that soar. Just as a breeze will fan a flame, so may friendship keep alive the spark of love between Brigid and Bran."

The officiant unfolds the satin cloth to reveal the rings. She sprinkles a drop of rose oil and a drop of sage oil on the cauldron-candle flame and then passes each ring over the flame to cleanse it. (When oil is used to produce smoke for ritual cleansing purposes, the smoke will fade before the object to be cleansed is passed over the flame; this is fine, since the cleansing is symbolic.) The officiant says, "These rings, forged in fire and cooled in air, are a symbol of love and life." The lovers extend their hands to receive each other's rings. Brigid places the ring on the fourth finger of Bran's left hand, saying, "Just as the circle represents eternity, so this ring is my promise to love you for a lifetime." Bran then places the ring on the fourth finger of Brigid's left hand, saying, "Just as the circle is never ending, so this ring is my promise to love you for all of my life."

The officiant raises a goblet of red wine and hands it to Brigid. She and Bran each take a sip and return the goblet to the officiant. The officiant says, "The element of water is represented in this goblet of red wine. May love flow always in this union, bringing to the partnership great compassion and spiritual depth."

Taking a small handful of sea salt and rose petals, the officiant then lets the mixture fall to the earth at the couple's feet. The officiant says, "Sea salt and rose petals represent the element earth. May this union be blessed with a strong and steadfast foundation of love that is pure." Addressing the guests, the officiant declares, "Let all acknowledge the commitment that this couple makes to each other here today. Now Brigid and Bran will exchange vows."

Brigid and Bran turn to face each other. First Brigid recites her personal vows, then Bran recites his. They turn back to the officiant, who sprinkles a drop of rose oil on the cauldron candle flame, followed by a drop of sage oil.

The officiant says to the groomsman, "May I have the cords, please?" The groomsman gives the cords to the officiant, and she passes them above the candle to cleanse them. As the cords are cleansed, the couple steps back far enough to allow the maid and groomsman to take a position before the altar. The officiant hands the cords to the maid and groomsman. With a simple twist (explained in the Cords section of chapter 4), the maid and groomsman create the infinity symbol.

The officiant says to Brigid and Bran, "Please extend your right hands." The couple extends their hands, and the maid and groomsman slip the infinity loop over their wrists. The officiant requests that Brigid and Bran turn to each other and clasp hands. They join hands.

The officiant says, "Brigid, do you promise to cherish Bran, to pledge to him your love and your support for all of this lifetime?" *Brigid answers.*

"Brigid, do you accept the commitment that this cord symbolizes, a commitment to be bound to each other as one for all of this life?" *Brigid answers.*

The officiant then says, "Bran, do you promise to cherish Brigid, to pledge to her your love and your support for all of this life time?" *Bran answers.*

"Bran, do you accept the commitment that this cord symbolizes, a commitment to be bound to each other as one for all of this life?" *Bran answers.*

The officiant places her hand on the couple's clasped hands and says, "Let all witness the union of this loving couple. Know that these cords are but a symbol. In truth, these two lovers bind each other, one unto the other. The cords will be removed, but the union of their hearts and spirits is one they freely choose." The officiant then removes her hand. The maid and the groomsman remove the cords and place them on the altar.

Addressing the guests, the officiant announces, "Friends and family of Brigid and Bran, you are the witnesses to the declarations made here today. Brigid and Bran have chosen this sacred union and promise to cherish and protect each other and their precious love. In the heat of every ember's spark, in the fragrant breath of every gently blowing breeze, in the gurgling of every brook, and in the majesty of a snow-laden mountain range, there is the design of Nature. Today, Brigid and Bran follow their destiny and join their lives. They came to us today as two. They leave here today as one. Let all of us give our true affection and support to this couple. So mote it be."

The couple kiss. The officiant says, "Please stand," and rings a bell three times before declaring, "I announce to all that Brigid and Bran are united as one, and I introduce you to the handfasted couple."

The couple join hands and jump the broom. The guests applaud. The couple continues their exit. The maid lifts the broom and steps back to link arms with the groomsman. The maid and groomsman follow the couple out.

Variations

There are many ways that you can adapt this ceremony to conform to your personal preferences. This section explores how to modify your handfasting to include parents and/or children; it also offers suggestions for those who would prefer to do without an officiant and those interested in a more Witchcraft or Wiccan-oriented handfasting.

One important thing to consider if you will be including children from previous unions in your ceremony is their availability. If you have any doubts that they will be able to attend — they may feel uncomfortable, or there may be custody issues involved — then find some way to include them in the union that doesn't require them to be at the hand-fasting; for example, recognize them in the symbolism of your ring design by using their birthstones in the setting.

If you are certain that the children will be with you on your special day, then their ages become a factor in your planning. If the children are older, you can decide together what part they could play in the ritual; but if they are younger than thirteen, keep their part simple and nonessential. In the sample ceremony described earlier, the maid could hold the children's hands, and one of the children could carry the broom. Ornate cushions could be set at either side of the altar for the children to sit on, after they have been led there by the maid.

If your parents have dreamed of seeing you married in a church cer-emony, you may decide to at least accommodate the "father of the bride" by inviting him to walk his daughter down the aisle. The sim-plest way to adapt the sample ceremony to this purpose is to have the groomsman and groom enter and stand to the right of the altar. Then have the bride and her father come down the aisle, led by the maid. Continue with the ritual as described once the couple have joined one another at the altar.

Another way to involve parents is to replace the section of the sam-ple ceremony beginning with, "The officiant asks the guests to stand," and ending with, "They will now light the unity candle to symbolize their wish to join as one." Use the following scenario, instead. When the harpist pauses, the officiant announces, "We will begin." First, Brigid's parents walk down the aisle and stand at the altar while the of-ficiant lights Brigid's individual candle (since parents are often more nervous than their marrying child, it is best to have someone else light the candle). The officiant says, "Let this candle symbolize the unique individuality of Brigid and the loving family that supports her here

THE CEREMONY: YOUR VOWS & RITUAL ∞ 167

today." The parents then step back to the left, out of the circle, and await their daughter.

Next, Bran's parents walk down the aisle and stand at the altar while the officiant lights Bran's individual candle. The officiant says, "Let this candle symbolize the unique individuality of Bran and the loving family that supports him here today." The parents then step back to the right, out of the circle, and await their son.

Only then does the officiant ask the guests to stand. The harpist resumes playing. The groomsman leads the procession, the couple walking side by side, groom on the right, bride on the left. The maid follows, carrying the broom. The groomsman enters the circle and stands to the right of the altar. Brigid and Bran pause to hug their respective parents, then the parents take their seats. The couple enters the circle and stands directly before the altar; Bran stands to the right, Brigid to the left. The maid follows and stands to Brigid's left.

The officiant says, "Welcome all to the handfasting of Brigid and Bran. You may sit." The officiant continues, "We come to this sacred place with our hearts full of hope and good wishes for this couple's happy union. The maid will now close the circle with the ceremonial broom." The maid sweeps once and then places the broom across the circle's opening.

Dipping the stir stick into a vessel of sage oil, the officiant lets a few drops fall on the flame of a candle burning inside a pewter cauldron, saying, "This circle is purified with sage and has been swept clean so that only positive natural energies remain. The parents of Brigid and Bran have lit candles for their children. Brigid and Bran have come to this sacred site as two. They will now light the unity candle to symbolize their wish to join as one." The ritual then continues as described in the sample ceremony section.

If the parent/s in question are on one side only—that is, if they are the bride's *or* the groom's—you may want to discuss ways of involving them that don't highlight the absence of the other set of parents. The key is to give them a task or position that does not need to be balanced by another set of parents; or, if the parents have a genuine affection for both the bride and groom, they can act for both in the ritual. Here is a list of possible solutions:

- Ask the attending parent/s to give a short reading.
- Arrange special seating for them at the ceremony.
- Have the procession pause briefly at the seat of the parent/s in attendance and give them a quick kiss without asking them to stand (this will seem spontaneous, and it eclipses the need for a balanced display).
- Balance the parent/s of one partner with dear friend/s of the other.
- Have the parent/s join the procession behind the couple and in front of the maid. Before the party enters the circle, allow the parent/s to kiss both the bride and the groom before taking their seats.
- If a parent is not present because she or he has passed on, then offer that parent a ceremonial libation.
- Make a special toast to the parent/s at the celebration.

Should you and your partner choose the no-officiant variation, you should plan a very simple ceremony, perhaps as short as fifteen minutes. But this does not mean that your handfasting experience will be anything less than rich and meaningful.

Since this type of ritual is likely to contain fewer symbolic elements, it makes sense to devote extra effort to the decor, your attire, and the celebration afterwards. Through these elements, you can communicate what this union means to you as a couple. Do not push yourselves into performing a complex ritual or reciting long vows. You are making memories at your handfasting; let them be joyous ones.

Browse through the preceding chapters again, and focus on elements that you can work with outside of the ceremony. For example, think about creating a beautiful ceremonial circle of herbs and wildflowers that will convey great meaning. Or save the broom jumping for the celebration—it's great fun for your guests to see you jump the broom as you leave the festivities and head home for the first time as a hand-fasted couple. Perform such ritual tasks as consecrating the rings, puri-fying the circle, or performing the elemental blessings over the cords before the ceremony, and then wrap cleansed objects in white cloth.

Consider using this adaptation of the sample ceremony: A flutist is playing as the guests arrive. When all are seated, the flutist pauses, then begins a significantly different piece of music as a way to announce to the guests that the ceremony is about to begin.

In front of the guests is the ceremonial circle. Inside it, candles are burning and a censer is emitting fragrant smoke. Towards the north of the circle, there is a focal point—perhaps an altar (a small one), or something that doesn't even resemble a table, such as an arched trellis, a large rock, or an oak tree. For this particular adaptation, envi-sion a white marble column, about three feet tall. On this altar sit the rings, folded into white satin, and the cords, neatly coiled around the perimeter.

The groomsman leads the procession, the couple walking side by side, groom on the right, bride on the left, behind the groomsman. The maid follows. (If the bride and groom have written out their vows, then the maid and the groomsman carry these in white leather folders.) The groomsman enters the circle and stands behind the altar. The couple enters and stands at either side of the altar (bride to the left, groom to the right) so that the guests see them in profile. The maid stands to the left of the bride and beside the groomsman.

Brigid turns to the guests and says, "Bran and I welcome you to our handfasting. Please sit." Bran turns to the guests and adds, "We come to this sacred place in perfect love and perfect trust, with our hearts full of hope and with the wish to be united." The couple turns back to face each other across the altar. Brigid unfolds the cloth to reveal the rings.

As Brigid places the ring on Bran's finger, she says, "Just as the circle represents eternity, so this ring is my promise to love you for a lifetime." As Bran places the ring on Brigid's finger, he says, "Just as the circle is never ending, so this ring is my promise to love you for all of my life." If the groomsman and the maid are carrying the vows, they now hand them to the couple. The groomsman and the maid lift the cords and twist them once to form the infinity symbol.

Brigid recites the vows she has written and places her folder on the altar. Bran recites the vows he has written and places his folder on the altar. The couple raises their right arms and extends them across the altar. The maid and the groomsman slip the infinity loop over their wrists. The couple clasps right hands.

Brigid says, "With these cords, I choose to be bound to Bran for the rest of my life." Bran says, "With these cords, I choose to be bound to Brigid for the rest of my life." The maid and the groomsman remove the cords and place them on the altar. Bran and Brigid step towards one another and kiss. They turn to the audience. Hand in hand, they address their guests in unison: "We would like to thank our friends and family for joining us today. You are the witnesses to our love and to our pledge. Thank you for your love and support."

Brigid and Bran exit, followed by the maid and the groomsman, who have first picked up the vows, the cords, and the ring cloth.

Those of you who are involved in Witchcraft or Wicca may wish to adapt the sample ceremony, as well. First, you will need to arrange for the services of a high priestess and/or a high priest, depending upon your coven's practices. Next, follow the circle-casting directions given in chapter 5, Sacred Space and Divination, to mark your handfasting space. This adapted ceremony will commence once the swirling energies of the elementals surround you, the handfasting couple, and the presence of the divine is felt in the sacred space. At this point, the high priestess (in this example) will summon the Goddess and the God using this invocation:

APHRODITE
Glorious lady of beauty and desire
Great Goddess who kindles passion's hot fire
Moon Queen who rules fertility
Whose wisdom knows love's mystery
Come to us to witness this rite
Where lovers have chosen this day to unite.

ADONIS
Magnificent lord of youth and desire
Great God whose potency is creation's fire
In your strength and virility
With your brilliant divinity
Join with us this handfasting to bless
For this couple bound by love and tenderness.

The couple stands at the altar, facing north. The priestess picks up a small handful of sea salt and rose petals. She lets the mixture fall to the earth at the couple's feet. The priestess says, "Power of earth this union bless with strength and love and happiness. So mote it be." (Here you may insert additional words from the sample ceremony, if appropriate.)

The couple then turns to the east. The priestess drops rose oil and sage oil on the flames of a candle burning in a pewter cauldron and uses a feather to symbolically catch the smoke and swirl it towards the couple. As she does so, she says, "Power of air this union bind with thoughts of sharing and gestures kind. So mote it be." (Here you may insert additional words from the sample ceremony.) The couple turns back to the altar.

The priestess hands each a white candle to be lit from the cauldron candle. Brigid and Bran light their respective candles. Turning towards the south, they raise their candles. The priestess says, "Power of fire this union fashion with inspiration and love's true passion. So mote it be." (Here you may insert additional words from the sample ceremony.) The couple returns the candles to the altar.

The priestess hands Brigid a goblet of wine. The couple turn to the west. Brigid sips, then passes the goblet to Bran, who also sips. The priestess says, "Power of water this union bless with deep compassion and tenderness. So mote it be." (Here you may insert additional words from the sample ceremony.) Bran hands the goblet back to the priestess.

Unfolding the satin cloth, the priestess reveals the rings. She places a drop of rose oil and a drop of sage oil on the cauldron-candle flame and passes each ring over the flame to cleanse it. The priestess says, "O Great Goddess, we ask that you bless these rings, sacred circles from which eternity springs. Here a lifetime commitment these lovers make, their bond to each other ne'er to forsake."

Brigid recites the vows she has written; Bran recites the vows he has written. Taking a small handful of sea salt and rose petals, the priestess sprinkles the mixture on the handfasting cords as a gesture of purification. She lets a few drops of rose oil and sage oil fall on the cauldron-candle flame, passes the cords through the smoke, and hands the cords to the maid and the groomsman. They twist the cords into the infinity symbol. The couple extends their right arms, and the maid and the grooms-man slip the infinity loop over their wrists. The couple clasps hands.

The priestess says, "Brigid and Bran, this cord does bind, body, heart, soul, and mind, join now in love, in harmony grow, as above, so below. So mote it be. Here, before witnesses, do you make this pledge?" Brigid and Bran answer. The priestess continues, "Know that these cords are but a symbol. In truth, these two lovers bind each other, one unto the other. The cords will be removed, but the union of their hearts and spirits is one they freely choose." The maid and the groomsman remove the cords and place them on the altar. The priestess raises the chalice and dips the athame deep into the liquid, declaring, "May your love honor the Lord and the Lady always."

The lovers kiss. The maid places the broom in the couple's path, and the couple jumps the broom.

Finally, here is one small variation that has become quite popular: you and your partner prick your index fingers of your right hands and mingle blood as part of the ritual. The symbolism is wonderful, particularly when you are binding for a lifetime or eternity. But, as always, there is a practical side to consider. The symbol of a white dress smeared with blood is probably not part of your vision. If you are going to do this, try it out in advance. Also, plan to perform this symbolic act at a point in the ceremony when you won't be needing your hands;

you'll have to apply pressure to the pricked finger with your thumb until the bleeding stops. If you want to use a ceremonial dagger as the puncturing instrument, be very careful not to slice yourselves. A pearl-headed pin, available at millinery or bridal shops, is perhaps a better choice. Or, prick your fingers just before the ceremony, put a drop or two in a little dish, and add a touch of water. During the ceremony, have the officiant dip the dagger into the blood and dab it on each of your fingers; then press your fingers together.

There are many elements that you may add to your handfasting ceremony that will make it meaningful to you as a couple. Chances are, you will come up with all kinds of romantic ideas. Be careful, however, not to take on more than you can handle. And select elements that complement each other so that your ritual will flow along naturally. Whatever you choose, remember to ask yourself practical questions before you commit to your choices: What do I need? How will it work? Who will do what?

The handfasting ceremony should reflect you as a couple. Set the tone, choose the appropriate symbolic elements, and create a day full of special significance. Take your time, and make your day romantic, meaningful, and truly magickal.

IN CONCLUSION

Enjoy your special day. Fill your union with magick and meaning. Know that your love is a force of Nature and your bond is a sacred oath. By hand-fasting, you choose to make a commitment to the one you love through ceremony and celebration. Be inspired by the ancients and guided by the divine. Let the magick swirl around you. And let Nature, in all her glory, be a part of all your days, ever after. Remain filled with the wonder that lovers throughout time have found in their sacred unions.

⊠ ⊠ ⊠

Long ago, but not so far away

A bride lingered at a clearing's edge.

Pink petals from apple blossom trees flittered through the air

And were gently dusted from her shoulders by her wee bridesmaids.

In those days, the bride was known to be attended by faeries.

⊠ ⊠ ⊠

Selected
Bibliography

Amt, Emilie, ed. *Women's Lives in Medieval Europe: A Sourcebook*.
London: Routledge, 1993.

Ball, Pamela. *The Complete Dream Dictionary*. Toronto: Prospero, 2000.

Bosworth, Joseph, and T. Northcote Toller. *An Anglo-Saxon Dictionary*.
London: Oxford UP, 1964.

Bowersock, G.W., ed. *Philostratus: Life of Apollonius*. Trans. C.P. Jones.
Harmondsworth: Penguin, 1970.

Brodribb, W.J., and A.J. Church, trans. *Complete Works of Tacitus*. New
York: Random, 1942.

Campbell, Joseph. *The Hero with a Thousand Faces*. New York: MJF,
1949.

Campbell, Josie P. *Popular Culture in the Middle Ages*. Bowling Green:
Bowling Green State U Popular P, 1986.

Clark, Kenneth. *Civilization*. London: B.B.C., 1980.

Cotterell, Arthur. *The Encyclopedia of Mythology*. London: Lorenz,
1999.

Cunningham, Scott, and David Harrington. *Living Wicca*. St. Paul:
Llewellyn, 1990.

de Vore, Nicholas. *Encyclopedia of Astrology*. Totowa: Littlefield, 1976.

Dolnick, Barrie. *Simple Spells for Love*. New York: Harmony, 1994.

Duby, George. *Love and Marriage in the Middle Ages*. Chicago: U of
Chicago P, 1988.

Dunwich, Gerina. *Wicca A to Z*. Secaucus: Citadel, 1997.

Gies, Frances, and Joseph Gies. *Life in a Medieval Village*. New York: Harper, 1990.

Grist, Aileen, and Tony. *Wicca*. New York: Sterling, 2000.

Hogue, John. *Nostradamus: The Complete Prophecies*. London: Element, 1997.

Kinney, Jay, and Richard Smoley. *Hidden Wisdom: A Guide to the Western Inner Traditions*. New York: Penguin, 1999.

Kuhn, Sherman M., ed. *Middle English Dictionary*. Ann Arbor: U of Michigan P, 1997.

Lawless, J. *The Encyclopedia of Essential Oils*. London: Element, 1992.

Maxwell-Hudson, C. *The Complete Book of Massage*. London: Dorling-Kindersley, 1990.

Meyer, Michael. *A Handbook for the Humanistic Astrologer*. Garden City: Anchor, 1974.

Mikkers, Bote. *The Pendulum Workbook*. Bath: Ashgrove, 1990.

Pennick, Nigel. *The Complete Illustrated Guide to Runes*. London: Element, 1999.

Pope, John C., ed. *Seven Old English Poems*. London: Norton, 1981.

Rabey, Steve. *In the House of Memory*. New York: Penguin, 1998.

Raphaell, Katrina. *Crystal Enlightenment*. Santa Fe: Aurora, 1985.

Scott, Sir Walter. *The Monastery*. London: Dent, 1969.

Starhawk. *The Spiral Dance*. San Francisco: HarperCollins, 1979.

—. *Dreaming the Dark*. Boston: Beacon, 1982.

Telesco, Patricia. *Wicca 2000*. Secaucus: Citadel, 1999.

—. *The Wiccan Book of Ceremonies and Rituals*. Secaucus: Citadel, 1999.

Urlin, Ethel L. *A Short History of Marriage*. Detroit: Singing Tree, 1969.

Warner, Rex, ed. *Encyclopedia of World Mythology*. London: Peerage, 1975.

Wildwood, Chrissie. *Aromatherapy*. London: Bloomsbury, 1996.

Index

105, 118, 119, 128, 158, 169; Sacred tree, 21; Symbolism, 80-81; Tree Astrology, 33-35; Tree of Life, 33

Unity Candle. *See* Candle

Variations on Ceremony, 165-174
Venus, 35, 36, 37, 43, 44, 46, 83, 87, 91, 96, 106, 147
Vocabulary, 160-161
Vow book, 57, 71, 73, 169
Vows (*See also* Vow Book): in Ceremony, 22, 125, 153-54, 163, 171, 173; Choosing and Writing Vows, 108, 154-61
Wand, 115, 120-21, 123, 125, 129
Water. *See* Elements
Wicca, 102, 127, 165, 171
Witchcraft, 14, 22, 83, 125, 165, 171
Wordsworth, William, 13

Zodiac (*See also* Astrology), 35, 37, 45, 142-46; Zodiac Signs, 148-51; Zodiac Signs and Rulership Chart, 35, 36